H ow do adults grow in their faith while living in a modern world in which people are increasingly detached from religion? How do we pastoral ministers help them do that? In this excellent and basic book, Jane Regan provides a road map to help us examine this and plan ways to succeed. Her chapter on helping adults enter into conversations about faith is alone worth the price of this book.

BILL HUEBSCH, *author of Dreams and Visions: Pastoral Planning for Lifelong Faith Formation (New London, CT: Twenty-Third Publications, 2010)*

A s always, Jane Regan challenges as well as affirms, explores theory as well as realistic practice, and names the frustrations and hurdles as well as the vision and hopes for adult faith formation, evangelization, and, in reality, all of parish life.

Rooted in Scripture, in the way Jesus taught, in church documents on adult formation and evangelization, and based in our culture's postmodernity and the actual lives of today's parishioners, Jane takes us on a journey of renewed possibilities for adult faith formation and the very life of today's parish.

It's hard to believe that so much is contained in one short book. Jane pulls together an approach to the actual experiences of people's everyday faith life, the struggles and potentials of our parishes, and the promising opportunities of adult faith formation to help us receive new insights, challenges, and concrete, authentic practices. Unquestionably, this is an indispensable book for every staff member and every person in parish leadership. It provides much to reflect on, and Jane's suggested discussion questions will guide our conversations and make renewed adult faith formation come alive in our communities.

JANET SCHAEFFLER, OP, *author, adult fai*

D1572259

Welcome to the new world of adult faith formation! Jane Regan serves as our guide to this new world, blending theory and practice to help leaders bring adult faith formation to life in their parish communities. She examines the postmodern culture of our world today and outlines important implications for adult faith formation. She summarizes the major themes of the church's vision of evangelization and catechesis. She offers practical insights about building formal, structured programs that are informed by adult learning characteristics. And she shows how informal models of adult faith formation offer a variety of ways for a parish to develop or enhance their adult faith formation efforts. Jane has given us the vision and tools—now let's get moving and develop adult faith formation for this new world!

JOHN ROBERTO, *author,* ***Faith Formation 2020*** *and* ***Reimagining Faith Formation for the 21st Century***

Forming a Community of Faith

FORMING A COMMUNITY OF *Faith*

A guide to success in adult faith formation today

JANE E. REGAN

TWENTY
THIRD 23rd
PUBLICATIONS
www.23rdpublications.com

Twenty-Third Publications

1 Montauk Avenue, Suite 200, New London, CT 06320

(860) 437-3012 » (800) 321-0411 » www.23rdpublications.com

ISBN: 978-1-62785-023-0

Library of Congress Catalog Card Number: 2014935250

Printed in Canada

CONTENTS

WELCOME ix

CHAPTER ONE 1

Context for Forming
an Adult Community

CHAPTER TWO 17

Evangelization and the Call
for Adult Catechesis

CHAPTER THREE 39

Forming Adult Faith

CHAPTER FOUR 63

Adults Engaged in Conversations
that Matter

CHAPTER FIVE 83

Community of Practice as Agent
of Faith Formation

NOTES 102

MY OWN INTEREST IN ADULT FAITH FORMATION CAN BE traced back to my earliest involvement in religious education. From the first parish I worked in as a DRE in the mid-1970s, I've recognized the importance of engaging adults as the primary participants in parish faith formation. As I continued to be involved in adult faith formation at the parish and diocesan level along the East Coast and in the Midwest, my conviction continued to grow that the religious education of children and youth, always essential to the life of the parish, is best understood and most effectively implemented in a context where priority is given to the faith formation of the adults. It is in light of that belief that this book was written.

This book is addressed to those whose interests and ministry focus on the faith formation of adults. Central themes of adult faith formation—evangelization, catechesis, conversation, community—are woven throughout the text, interspersed with lots of examples and practical suggestions. The "Keep in Mind" at the end of each chapter provides a summary of some of the core ideas and concepts explored in the chapter.

While it can certainly be read on your own, it is also helpful to use with a group of people—adult educators from neighboring parishes, religious education advisory boards, or an adult education team. There are questions at various points in each chapter that are helpful for reflection and conversation; they are designed to both enhance your understanding of the text and foster your own growth in faith—because that is, in fact, where our interests lie—strengthening our own faith and the faith of those around us. I wish you all the best in that!

CHAPTER ONE

Context for Forming an Adult Community

WHICH ARE YOUR FAVORITE STORIES ABOUT JESUS, YOUR favorite pericopes or sections from the gospels that speak to you about who Jesus was? Perhaps it is one of the stories he told, or an account of a miracle event. Or maybe it is a description of how he responded to people's questions or to the challenges from the religious leaders. Take a moment and think of your top three or four. Looking at these accounts from Jesus' life gives us a sense of *how* Jesus taught and *what* he taught to those who followed him.

At the heart of this book is the question of how adults grow in their faith. From the perspective of the religious educator, we can ask it this way: how do we form adults within the Christian faith? We can set out the parameters of our response to that question by asking, "What would it mean to teach as Jesus did?" We are not the first to pose this question. In fact, in the 1980s, a church document that addressed catechesis was entitled "To Teach as Jesus Did." Although this document was addressed primarily to the needs of adolescent catechesis, it seems to me that the title is an apt one and points to a good place to begin thinking about how we form adults within the Christian faith.

In this chapter, we examine two significant themes. The first one involves looking back to the gospels and to the life of the early church and examining the models of teaching that Jesus embodied and the way that was understood by his followers. The second theme is a "yes, but" response to the first: yes, we want Jesus' example to inspire our work, but our cultural context is very different from first-century Judaism. So we ask about the challenges and gifts that elements of twenty-first-century American culture bring to the way in which we give expression to Jesus' example. And we conclude this chapter by setting out the key moves that make up the remainder of the book.

To Teach as Jesus Did...

It is a bit glib and somewhat too simplistic to repeat the oft-made comparison: Jesus welcomed the children but taught the adults, and the church has been doing just the opposite for years. But there is a truth to that. If we examine most parishes' investment of time, talent, and financial resources in service to faith formation, we would generally see that a good deal of emphasis is placed on children and youth, with little attention given to adults. And often the segment that is addressed to adults is primarily designed to help them be more effective ministers or catechists or parents and is only secondarily addressed to their own faith formation as adult believers. But we see in Jesus' life, as we come to know it through the gospels, that the calling and forming of adult followers was at the heart of his ministry.

At the beginning of his ministry, as told in Matthew's gospel, for example, Jesus called Simon and Andrew to leave their nets and follow him, that he would make them "fishers of men" (4:18–19).[1] He then set about teaching those who followed him, "proclaiming the gospel of the kingdom, and curing every disease and illness among the people" (4:23). And the Gospel of Matthew concludes with Jesus sending the disciples out to teach others: "Go, therefore, and make disciples of all nations, baptizing them in the name of the Father, and of the Son, and of the Holy Spirit, teaching them to observe all that I have commanded you. And behold, I am with you always, until the end of the age" (28:19–20). So Jesus' actions of calling and sending bracket the whole of Matthew's gospel; between these two actions, Jesus taught through word and deed both the substance of a new world view and the way of life that flowed from it.

If we look at the *way* Jesus taught, it is clear what Jesus *didn't* do; he didn't lecture or outline abstract concepts. He taught in parable—the kingdom of God is like a king who planned a great feast, or a farmer who planted a field, or a woman who lost a coin.[2] And he taught in story—there once was a man with two sons, or a shepherd with a hundred sheep, or a man going down from Jerusalem to Jericho who fell among thieves.[3] Jesus answered questions—"What must I do to attain eternal life?" or "Which is the greatest commandment?" or "How many times must I forgive my brother?" And he addressed people in the midst of their lives—Zaccheus, as he climbed a tree to get a better view, the Samaritan woman who had gone to the well to draw water, and the woman who wished to be healed by merely touching the hem of his cloak.

At the same time, if we look at *what* Jesus taught, we recognize that he *didn't* teach propositions or discrete doctrines. Jesus taught most effectively by example—by gathering his disciples for meals, by welcoming the sinners, and by healing those who were brought to him. He taught a way of life by challenging the status quo and by taking time away by himself for prayer or with his disciples in order to explain to them more deeply the truth that he was living and the consequence of that truth.

Ultimately, the disciples learned by entering into an apprenticeship with Jesus. They travelled with him, listened to him as he taught, and watched as he healed people. At some point they were sent out in pairs to do the same, reporting back to Jesus about their success and questions.[4] They grew in their understanding of, and capacity for, being a disciple of Jesus by following his example, by doing what he did.

So to "teach as Jesus did" is to set out a vision and a way of life. Through story and conversation, through example and shared interactions, we convey to others the meaning of the reign of God and we witness to a life shaped by gospel values. In sum, to use the words of Peter in his first letter, we are called to "always be ready to give an explanation to anyone who asks you for a reason for your hope" (1 Peter 3:15).

Let me propose that this gives an overall sense of what we are about in adult faith formation. Certainly we want to teach about the faith, but more importantly, we want to foster faith in ourselves and in those with and for whom we minister. This is what the early followers of Jesus did; this is what they understood by the injunction to make disciples and teach what Jesus had commanded. The vision of the community set out in the Acts of the Apostles points to that type of teaching and witnessing:

They devoted themselves to the teaching of the apostles and to the communal life, to the breaking of the bread and to the prayers. Awe came upon everyone, and many wonders and signs were done through the apostles. All who believed were together and had all things in common; they would sell their property and possessions and divide them among all according to each one's need. Every day they devoted themselves to meeting together in the temple area and to breaking bread in their homes. [**ACTS 2:42–46**]

We know from reading the rest of the New Testament that there were challenges to this description. There were debates over the reception of the Gentiles; there were problems with people not sharing things in common; there were even debates about who taught what to whom. But through all that, the lasting challenge to live in love and hope allowed the early followers of Jesus and the nascent church to survive and thrive against all odds.

Questions for Reflection and Conversation

⋆ *Reflect back on one of the gospel pericopes you named at the beginning of the chapter. What aspect of the story points to how and what Jesus taught? What implications does this have for your own teaching?*

⋆ *When you hear the phrase "to teach as Jesus did," what image or experience or approach comes to mind? In what ways is this a helpful way to think about your own teaching?*

⋆ *What do you see as some of the challenges to responding to the call "to teach as Jesus did"?*

...In the Twenty-First Century

Yes, to teach as Jesus did is an important and helpful vision, *but* how do we translate that into our twenty-first-century context? Even describing our contemporary culture and getting a handle on the social, political, economic, and religious dynamics that shape the way in which we approach adult faith formation is a task that far exceeds the scope of this book or any one text. The most we can do is pick up one lens as a way of looking at our contemporary context, one lens that sheds light on our work as religious educators of adults.

The lens I want to pick up is that of "postmodernity." Whether or not you are familiar with that term, you'll recognize some of the examples that mark a postmodern context:

- The number of people who say that they are "spiritual but not religious."

- The plethora of books designated "spirituality" with no coherent way to sort them out. One of the big chains labels this section: "Spirituality/New Age: Arranged Alphabetically by Author."

- The popularity of "reality TV" with its emphasis on the life of a particular person or group of people.

- The recognition that irreducible pluralism is not only a reality, but may in fact be a benefit to culture and society.

While cultural postmodernity is a complex and multifaceted reality, it is possible to propose some key characteristics that permeate the concept.[5]

The first characteristic of postmodernity is the self-conscious recognition that human knowing is defined in space and time. The way we perceive reality and come to understand ourselves and the world around us is shaped by our place in history and society. I see and understand the world as a Catholic woman living in the eastern United States in the first decades of the twenty-first century. My "situatedness"—my past history and my present experience—shapes how I perceive everything from the mundane to the deeply philosophical, from what I understand to be appropriate clothes for work to how I construe the meaning of freedom or independence.

An example: when my children were growing up, my older daughter went to school in a neighboring town that was about 65% Jewish. Many of the kids she spent time with, and a high number of the teachers and staff at her school, were Jewish. At the same time, the neighborhood where we lived had the look of a meeting of the UN. The young couple who lived next door to us was from India; we regularly profited from their traditional cooking around their holidays. And on the other side was a family who emigrated from Russia. Across the way were a couple of Muslim families with women and older girls wearing head coverings. The pluralism of my daughters' world and how they see and define the other is particularly evident when I reflect on my own growing up. The "other" for me was the Polish Catholic who went to St. Stanislaus while we, the Irish Catholics, went to St. Thomas. Or at most, it was the Presbyterians, who had a small church at the end of our street. There seemed to be clear, communally held lines between us and others, lines that have not been as clear for my daughters. They have grown up surrounded by people with different values and beliefs than they have; that is part of how they see reality today. For me, I came to the recognition of this pluralism as an adult and so experience it differently: I know of a time when diversity and pluralism did not define my world. My daughters have only known a world marked by pluralism—they think that that is the way it should be, the way it has always been. We each define and make meaning of the world in light of our own experience, our own situatedness.

What does this characteristic of cultural postmodernity say about how we think about adult faith formation as we strive to teach as Jesus did? One of the most important implications is the recognition that human experience serves as the starting point of adult catechesis. Effective adult catechesis draws on the experience of being a believer, shaped by the specific time and place, and sees those experiences as revelatory. The postmodern awareness of the way in which our human knowing is constructed within a specific time and place necessitates this renewed attention to methodology rooted in human experience.

Adult faith formation within a postmodern context means taking seriously the present reality of lived adult faith and providing people with the opportunity to reflect on that and talk about it with other adults. With this comes the recognition that people's experiences and views of the world vary considerably. When we take seriously human experience as the beginning point of adult catechesis, we recognize the irreducible pluralism within and outside our community. Our faith is enhanced when we engage this diversity and learn from it.

A second characteristic of postmodernity centers on the attitude toward "metanarratives." Metanarratives are the overarching stories we tell ourselves that help us make sense of the world. They can be rooted in family or community life—"That is not what Regans do," my father would remind us kids from time to time. They can also be socially or culturally formed. For example, in the United States, we put an emphasis on "rugged individualism" and the notion that if you work hard you will get ahead. Or we speak about the "American dream" of owning your own home as a sign of accomplishment and stability. For the person operating from a postmodern perspective, these metanarratives are looked upon with suspicion. This is particularly true when they are applied to large groups of people. The problem with metanarratives, from a postmodern perspective, is that they put forth overarching stories that ignore or even suppress alternative understandings or dissenting stories. At times metanarratives give stories of the collective to the loss of the individual's experience. And they can serve to sustain the status quo and the influence of large institutions. From a postmodern perspective, metanarratives are viewed with suspicion and with a sense that they should not be the starting point for how we make meaning in our lives. In the end it is not the metanarrative that will explain who we are and how we are to be: it is the individual's struggle to make meaning of his or her life.

Take, for example, a parish in a small farming community that was founded by European Catholics. The stories they tell about themselves and their parish highlight the sacrifice and dedication of the early members—the present parishioners' grandparents and great-grandparents. They have festivals and celebrations that mark feast days or special events. Early December, for example, is the time for the big Christmas bazaar that involves a significant number of the parishioners and takes a good deal of the parish's time and energy. These stories and events make up the metanarratives and rituals that define the community and provide a source of meaning for people's lives.

Now imagine that because of some light industry coming into the area, there is an influx of Latino/a Catholics into the parish. For them the prevailing metanarrative is foreign, even oppressive. For them early December is not time for a Christmas bazaar but the opportunity to celebrate the feast of Our Lady of Guadalupe, a central image to their own stories and sense of meaning. For this parish to become a parish of the descendants of original settlers and of the Latino/a community, the stories of the individuals involved need to take precedence over the dominant metanarrative in order to fashion a new, common story of what this community is about.

What are the implications of this for how we engage in adult faith formation? To be effective in forming an adult community, people need to be invited to tell their own stories and—in the telling, as well as in listening to the stories of others—to recognize the common themes that gather us as Christians. To tell one's story and to listen with an open heart to the story of others are skills that only come with practice. And yet it is only within these stories that we can trace out the common story—the Christian Story—that serves to give meaning to all of our individual narratives. In the final analysis we understand the paschal mystery as the source of meaning in our lives when we have gotten in touch with how new life comes from difficult or death-filled experiences in our own lives.

The third characteristic of a postmodern mindset is a tendency to be distrustful of large institutions. Large institutions are really the beneficiaries of the power of metanarratives to give meaning to a person's life. For example, if we believe in the metanarrative that modern (Western) medicine can heal all that ails us, then we are more likely to accept unquestioningly the doctor's advice and prescription and to undergo more willingly any tests and procedures that he or she recommends. The metanarrative keeps the medical industry flourishing. From a postmodern perspective, as with the metanarrative itself, the large institutions are looked at with some level of suspicion. They are recognized as human constructions and not the repository of omnipotent powers.

For us engaged in adult faith formation, it is important to grapple with the way in which the suspicion of large institutions applies to the church. Even for those of us whose affiliation with the church and involvement within its structures are perceived as "givens," we can have a questioning, critical, or suspicious stance toward elements of the institution. How much more so for those on the periphery of church life? In that context, it seems essential that the work we do in adult faith formation be always directed beyond the church boundaries. Our work with adults is to be oriented toward mission rather than simply toward membership or maintenance. To be an effective faith community in this postmodern context, deliberate attention needs to be given to mission over membership. We are rightly suspicious of charities where 40-50% of funds collected go to administrative costs rather than the charity's mission; administration is needed but must always be in service to mission. That same suspicion can be applied to a Christian community where most of its energy in faith formation of adults goes to enhance membership. We will look at this in more detail in the next chapter, but put simply, this means striving to be an evangelizing church, one that is always proclaiming the gospel in action and words, one that is always teaching as Jesus taught.

The fourth characteristic that marks a postmodern perspective is the heightened awareness of the place of power in social interactions. The recognition that knowledge and meaning are socially constructed and are rooted in an individual's (or group's) definition of their own situatedness, not in a metanarrative, leads to another recognition: those who define knowledge and meaning have social power. History is told by the winners. Those who tell the history, who decide what is important, are the ones with power. Power is not inherently good or bad, but it is power.

An example: the leadership of a moderate-size parish offered the opportunity for adults to gather in small groups for three sessions to discuss the place of liturgy in their lives. The organization was very good, with trained facilitators for each group of adults. The conversation for the first session went well, drawing on the experience of those present as well as liturgical documents for insight and direction. By the beginning of the second session, it became clear that the leadership had an agenda—building up support for the renovation of the church building—that had not been made clear at the start. Those in leadership had the power to set the agenda for these meetings. They also had the power to be transparent or not in their approach. But the participants had power as well: they could simply refuse to follow the set agenda. Power is present in all facets of our lives. The use of it in a faith-formation context needs to be carefully considered.

Effective adult catechesis in this postmodern setting engages in a model of catechesis that sees all of us as learners, all of us as apprentices to Jesus Christ. In this context, the stance of the teacher is key. How participants understand the role of teacher, the degree to which they see themselves as co-learners, the extent to which they recognize that there is wisdom already present in the community of faith, and the way in which hospitality and humility permeate the adult formation context: all of these contribute to a sense of the shared power of the group.

Within the postmodern context, people are looking to institutions like the church less as a source of answers and more as a place to give expression to their questions. Our role as religious educators is to provide the hospitable space where such inquiry can take place. It is enough that we invite the questions and then join with other adults to seek the responses.

Questions for Reflection and Conversation

★ *Where in your life have you encountered the currents of emerging postmodernity? How do you respond to these currents?*

★ *What are some of the signs of postmodernity present in the adults with whom you work? How do you respond to them?*

★ *What do you see as the challenges and promises for the church's response to this cultural shift?*

Map for the Journey

These two big themes—the challenge to teach as Jesus did and the reality of postmodernity—serve as framing elements to the rest of this book as we examine some of the essential components to the process of adult faith formation. To bring this chapter to conclusion, let me outline here the moves made in the remainder of the book.

Beginning with the General Catechetical Directory (GCD),[6] which was published in 1971, most ecclesial documents that discussed catechesis included the general sentiment reflected in this quote: "catechesis for adults, since it deals with persons who are capable of an adherence that is fully responsible, must be considered the chief form of catechesis. All the other forms, which are indeed always necessary, are in some way oriented to it" (GCD 20). So throughout the 1970s and beyond, the theme of the centrality of adult faith formation was regularly affirmed in official church documents. At the same time, ecclesial texts were being published that called for recognition of the centrality of evangelization to the mission of the church. *Evangelii Nuntiandi* (EN), The Apostolic Exhortation on Evangelization,[7] published by Pope Paul VI in 1975, states that the church "exists in order to evangelize" (EN 14). The essential role of evangelization in the nature and mission of the church can be found in church documents ever since.

My contention is that these two topics are linked, that there is a vital connection between the call to evangelization and the recognition of the necessity of the faith formation of adults. We explore this in chapter two. After examining the evolution of the understanding of evangelization from Vatican Council II to the present, as well as developing an understanding of "new evangelization," our attention turns to the essential link between evangelization and adult faith formation.

Given the central role of evangelization in the life of the church and to the work of catechesis, chapter three begins with a description of the interrelationship of evangelization, catechesis, and adult faith formation. It then proceeds to a discussion of what adult faith looks like. According to *Our Hearts Were Burning Within Us*, mature faith is living, explicit, and fruitful. In light of that understanding of faith, the goals of adult faith formation are examined and their implications for adult catechesis are explored.

Two major threads are considered as we look at faith formation of adults: the part played by various models of intentional programing and the role of the life of the community. On the one hand, intentional gatherings of adults specifically for formation, whether in peer groups or as part of multigenerational sessions, are an important part of the ongoing endeavor of adult catechesis. On the other hand, the very life of the parish is formative through its liturgy, service, and sense of community. Looking at these components, their contribution, challenges, and the interrelationship between them, is the focus of chapters four and five.

As discussed earlier in this chapter, the opportunity for adults to be in conversation with other adults about things that matter is at the heart of how adults grow in their faith. Hearing alternative views, listening to the faith stories of other people, articulating one's own understanding as clearly as possible: all of these are at the heart of the essential dynamic of adult faith formation—conversation. Chapter four looks at the nature of conversation, its role in adult catechesis, and the process of facilitating effective conversation. The last part of the chapter examines the important task of preparing and asking evocative and engaging questions, a skill that requires much practice.

Catechists meet to receive training, as do lectors; parish council members meet with the pastor to help him think through and make decisions about the pastoral life of the parish; the building committee meets to discuss repairs for the church building. Each of these groups meets for a specific task and agenda. But could these meetings be more? In the final chapter, we return to the role of the community as formative of faith, this time looking at the ways in which adults gather within a faith community and asking how these can be faith formative. We look at this through the lens of "communities of practice," proposing that the parish is a community of communities and that it is through our affiliation with these communities that our identity is formed and our faith fostered.

Keep in Mind

- In striving to teach as Jesus did, we look at both *how* Jesus taught (through stories and examples and addressing people's questions) and *what* he taught (a way of life).

- "Postmodernity" is one term used to describe our present complex, multidimensional cultural and social context.

- Postmodernity is characterized by recognition that human knowing is situated in time and place, that metanarratives are not the best way to explain a contemporary perspective or belief, that large institutions should be looked at with suspicion, and that power is present in all our social interactions.

- As we look at the theme of fostering adult faith, the concept of evangelization plays a significant role in understanding what we do and how we do it.

CHAPTER TWO

Evangelization and the Call for Adult Catechesis

ONE OF THE CONCEPTS EXPLORED IN THE LAST CHAPTER was the implication of following the injunction to "teach as Jesus did." In that context we examined *how* Jesus taught: he used stories and parables; he drew on people's lived experience and their own faith questions as the starting point of his teaching. And he taught by example, inviting his disciples into an apprenticeship with him. Addressing the same topic from another angle, we can ask about *what* Jesus taught. It is possible to list some things he taught—the Lord's Prayer, the Beatitudes, the greatest commandment—but what all of these items point to is the same single reality, the very heart of Jesus' teaching: the reign of God

In this chapter, we focus on evangelization, which in many ways is the same as saying that we are focusing on the reign of God, the heart of the gospel message. Pope Paul VI, in the apostolic exhortation *Evangelii Nuntiandi* (EN),[1] writes that "evangelizing means bringing the Good News into all the strata of humanity, and through its influence transforming humanity from within and making it new" (18). At a fundamental level, all Christians are called to be evangelizers. We are called to proclaim the gospel—the reign of God—in action and in word so that its truth, its visions and values, and its way of life can permeate all aspects of human existence.

At some level, one might ask: "When do I have the time to be an evangelizer? I am already overcommitted with work, parish, and family life." Ann, a theology teacher at a Catholic high school, might well ask that question. A typical day for Ann goes something like this: the morning is a rush of getting herself and her two kids out the door on time. Once she drops her children off at school, she takes the few moments of quiet afforded by the drive to the high school to center herself for the day. This morning she listens to the readings and reflection provided by "Pray-As-You-Go"[2] that is automatically downloaded to her iPhone each day. Arriving at school she checks her mail box and finds assorted announcements and a note from one of her students asking to meet with her during study period that afternoon. The day proceeds with each period being slightly shortened so that the monthly all-school Mass can take place after fifth period. While the shortened classes are a bit of a hassle for Ann, she appreciates the opportunity to participate in liturgy with this faith community. After Mass a student comes in to talk with her; what starts as a question about the class material evolves into a conversation about a family problem that the student is experiencing. Mostly, Ann listens, asks questions, and, as the conversation ends and the student is leaving, says simply "I'll keep you and your family in my prayers." After school Ann serves as coach for the girls' track team. When she first started being coach a few years back, she introduced the practice of beginning each team gathering with a moment of silent prayer. For the girls and for Ann, that is now a natural part of team practice. When she gets home from school, she finishes getting the supper ready that her husband had started, while he works with the kids on their homework. Suppertime is a special time for Ann and her family; it is about the only time all of them are gathered in one place for conversation. Both Ann and her husband are attentive to fostering a positive and affirming tone during the meal. After supper, Ann works on preparation for the next day's classes while the kids do homework and watch a bit of TV. When all head to bed, Ann is grateful for a good day.

So when does Ann have time to be an evangelizer? Actually, she already is. In her words and her actions; in how she relates to her family, students, and colleagues; in the integration of prayer and liturgy into her life; in the way she shows what she values in her actions: in all of these ways Ann is being an evangelizer to those around her. Enhancing Ann's awareness of this and deepening her capacity to live in a way that reflects gospel values is at the heart of the work of adult faith formation.

In this chapter, we look at what evangelization and the call to be an evangelizer looks like today by considering a series of church documents that examine the various components of our understanding of evangelization; all of these documents were issued in the years since Vatican Council II. The second section looks at the concept of "new evangelization": defining it and drawing out its implications for the life of the church and for adult faith formation in particular. In the final section of the chapter, we explore the relationship between the interest in evangelization and the attention given to adult faith formation. I believe that these two dynamics stem from a common charge: that we be and become an ever more effective evangelizing church.

Evangelization after Vatican Council II

As we examine the meaning and approach to evangelization in our contemporary context, we can do so by looking with care at a series of documents on evangelization that have been published since Vatican Council II. Beginning with *Ad Gentes*, a document of the Council that was promulgated in 1965, and continuing up through *Evangelii Gaudium*, prepared by Pope Francis in light of the discussion that took place at the synod on the new evangelization in 2012, the documents on evangelization and related topics weave together an understanding of evangelization that sets a hopeful and challenging vision for the church and all of its members.

A word about ecclesial documents: when talking about the dynamics of the pastoral life of the church, I have been heard to say on more than one occasion that "church documents are our friends!" Here I am particularly referring to those statements or exhortations pertaining to evangelization and catechesis. In what way are they "our friends"? First, documents in these areas often reflect a positive and constructive read of present cultural and ecclesial circumstances; at the same time they present a hopeful vision for the future of the church. For the most part, the documents maintain a balance between critiquing contemporary culture and recognizing the signs of grace within it. Second, they serve as helpful resources in tracing the evolution of a concept and the way in which the church has continued to develop in its understanding of various dynamics related to fostering faith. Comparing documents over time highlights the way in which concepts and approaches have responded to the contemporaneous context. And finally, as ecclesial documents, they serve as a sure foundation from which to proceed in developing pastoral plans. Reading church documents, discussing them with others, and reflecting on their application to your own setting are well worth the investment of time and energy.

For our discussion here, we are looking at six documents published between 1965 and 1998. In reading these documents, it is possible to see the evolution of thought on the nature of evangelization and a growing articulation of its place in the pastoral life of the church. It is beyond what we can do here to discuss these in detail; rather, for each of the documents I include a brief description of the source of the document and its fundamental focus. This is followed by highlighting a couple of the central contributions the document makes to our understanding of evangelization today.

We begin as much theological and pastoral discussion begins: with the documents of the Second Vatican Council. To some extent, many of the documents of Vatican II contribute to our understanding of evangelization, particularly those addressing the nature of the church: *Gaudium et Spes* (GS), The Church in the Modern World; and *Lumen Gentium* (LG), Dogmatic Constitution on the Church. These documents set out the ecclesiology that supports the vision of evangelization that has developed in subsequent years. But for our discussion, we look particularly at the document that addresses evangelization directly, the decree *Ad Gentes* (AG), On the Missionary Activity of the Church.[3]

Designed to set out the principles of missionary activity in the church, this document effectively reflects the understanding of mission and of evangelization operative at the time of the Council. While in many ways our understanding of evangelization has broadened since the writing of *Ad Gentes*, two themes are present in the document that find echo in later statements. The first is the recognition that evangelization is a complex reality, rooted in the culture and responsive to the needs of the setting. The document makes clear that there are three dimensions to it: witness through actions of charity and justice, proclamation, and establishing vibrant communities of faith. The second significant contribution of this document is its emphasis on the recognition that evangelization is the responsibility of all the members of the church: "the work of evangelization is a basic duty of the People of God" (35). And because of this, the formation of the laity is of utmost importance (21).

Ten years after the publication of *Ad Gentes* and the close of Vatican II, a synod of bishops was held in Rome specifically to address the topic of evangelization in the modern world. Following the synod, in 1975 Pope Paul VI presented *Evangelii Nuntiandi* (EN), the Apostolic Exhortation on Evangelization, which stands as an essential document for understanding evangelization today. Two key concepts run through the pages of the text. The first is that evangelization is of the very nature of the church. "Evangelizing is in fact the grace and vocation proper to the Church, her deepest identity. She exists in order to evangelize..." (14). This is the reason for the church's being—to be the agent of evangelization, which, as we saw earlier, means "bringing the Good News into all the strata of humanity, and through its influence transforming humanity from within and making it new" (18). Second, Pope Paul VI makes the point that the church is both evangelizer and always in need of evangelization (15). The ongoing renewal of the church is essential to its ability to fulfill God's fundamental mission for it—the mission to proclaim the gospel.

In 1977, another synod important to the development of our understanding of evangelization was held; this time the topic was catechesis, with particular attention to children and young people. Following the synod, Pope John Paul II issued *Catechesi Tradendae* (CT), the Apostolic Exhortation on Catechesis.[4] Reflective of the same vein of thought as EN, CT also affirms the centrality of evangelization to the life of the church. In CT, the multifaceted nature of evangelization is highlighted; Pope John Paul II speaks of various moments of evangelization: "Evangelization...is a rich, complex and dynamic reality, made up of elements, or one could say moments, that are essential and different from each other, and that must all be kept in view simultaneously" (18). He then goes on to say: "Catechesis is one of these moments—a very remarkable one—in the whole process of evangelization." Here evangelization is seen as being the foundation for the pastoral life of the church; all activities—preaching, liturgy, action for justice, community—make sense in light of the call to evangelize.

The next document comes ten years after CT. *Christifideles Laici* (CL), Apostolic Exhortation on the Laity,[5] was published in 1988 and is also the result of a synod of bishops that met, this time to discuss the role of the laity. CL is one of the first documents to introduce the concept of re-evangelization, later to be called new evangelization. Reflecting on the reality of de-Christianized contexts and the rise of secularism, Pope John Paul II calls for a re-evangelization, which begins with addressing the Christian community itself. We must "first remake the Christian fabric of the ecclesial community itself" so that it can reflect what it means to live in Christ (34). Members of the laity are essential participants in this task.

In 1991, Pope John Paul II promulgated the encyclical *Redemptoris Missio* (RM), On the Church's Mission Activity.[6]

This document included the clearest articulation of the meaning of "new evangelization" and the challenge that it holds for the church. While not wanting to lose focus on the responsibility of the church to proclaim the gospel to those who have never heard it (*ad gentes*), this document also makes the case for the importance of a new evangelization addressed to the baptized of all ages who have become distant from the church and Christ's teachings. One of the clarifying contributions of this document is the discussion of the three situations in which evangelization is needed. The first concerns "peoples, groups, and socio-cultural contexts in which Christ and his Gospel are not known, or which lack Christian communities sufficiently mature to be able to incarnate the faith in their own environment and proclaim it to other groups" (33). This is the classic understanding of evangelization *ad gentes*. The second situation focuses on the vibrant Christian communities that are able to support one another in the faith and provide a context where children can grow up in the faith. Here evangelization takes place in the regular pastoral life of the church. The third situation is "where entire groups of the baptized have lost a living sense of the faith, or even no longer consider themselves members of the Church, and live a life far removed from Christ and his Gospel. In this case what is needed is a 'new evangelization' or a 're-evangelization'" (33). We will return to this topic below.

The final document I want to mention is the *General Directory for Catechesis* (GDC),[7] published in 1998 by the Congregation for the Clergy, which has responsibility for overseeing catechesis.[8] In many ways, the GDC provides a good summative statement about the church's understanding of evangelization, weaving together many of the insights from the other documents we have examined. It is particularly compelling in its discussion of the multifaceted nature of evangelization and the various ways in which it comes to expression. It describes evangelization as "a dynamic reality which contains within it interdependent activities which are to be kept in creative tension: witness and proclamation, word and sacrament, interior change and social transformation" (46). The GDC develops in great detail the various expressions of evangelization and the centrality of catechesis, particularly adult catechesis, to the enterprise.

Latin title, DATE OF PUBLICATION ENGLISH TITLE	CONTRIBUTION
Ad Gentes (AG) 1965 DECREE ON MISSIONARY ACTIVITY IN THE CHURCH	■ three interrelated components: witness, proclamation, and establishing communities of faith ■ a strong laity is essential to evangelization
Evangelii Nuntiandi (EN) 1975 APOSTOLIC EXHORTATION ON EVANGELIZATION	■ the church exists in order to evangelize ■ the church is evangelizer and always in need of evangelization
Catechesi Tradendae (CT) 1977 APOSTOLIC EXHORTATION ON CATECHESIS	■ evangelization is multifaceted and complex ■ catechesis is a moment of evangelization
Christifideles Laici (CL) 1988 APOSTOLIC EXHORTATION ON THE LAITY	■ emphasis of the role of the laity ■ introduction of concept of re-evangelization

Redemptoris Missio (RM) 1991 Encyclical on the Church's Mission Activity	■ highlights importance of new evangelization ■ three contexts where evangelization is needed
General Directory for Catechesis (GDC) 1998	■ summary of previous documents

This brief foray into ecclesial documents related to evangelization provides a sense of the depth and complexity of the topic, and hopefully encourages readers to locate these documents—all of which are available free online—and review them for themselves. By way of integrating the insights of the documents, let me propose four general themes that develop across the texts.

EVANGELIZATION IS CONNECTED TO THE VERY LIFE AND IDENTITY OF THE CHURCH. It is of the very essence of the church to be about the sharing of the gospel with the world around us. While this may take various forms and formats depending on the life of the parish, a parish cannot simply shrug and say, "Well, we aren't really a welcoming community; we kind of stick together." Or parishioners cannot simply say, "I'm not comfortable sharing my faith," because the very way in which they live says something about the power of the gospel in their lives. To be a Christian community is to engage in evangelization.

EVANGELIZATION IS THE RESPONSIBILITY OF THE CHURCH AND ALL ITS MEMBERS. In the past, one thought of the church's evangelizing activity as something done by missionaries in faraway places. Our contemporary understanding has returned the responsibility for sharing the message of Christ to all believers, regardless of place or position. Particular emphasis is placed on the role of lay persons who through their jobs and families have the prime opportunity to witness to the reality of the reign of God by how they live their lives and engage with others around them.

EVANGELIZATION IS MULTIFACETED AND COMPLEX. It cannot be reduced to a certain set of tasks nor can it be assigned to a particular group within the parish. It has less to do with what the parish *does* and more with what the parish *is*. In this sense it might be more helpful to use the term "evangelizing": we can speak of evangelizing catechesis or evangelizing liturgy, an evangelizing youth group or an evangelizing finance committee, and ultimately an evangelizing parish. In each case, those responsible for these aspects of church life engage in their endeavors with an eye toward how their actions, attitudes, and decisions contribute to bringing the message of the reign of God into the world around us.

EVANGELIZATION IS ROOTED IN THE SITUATION OF THOSE BEING EVANGELIZED, particularly in terms of the new evangelization, as awareness of the situation of those being evangelized is key. How we address those who were baptized but never catechized is going to be different from those who were raised in the church and actively decided to leave. The evangelizing work done with young adults is different from that done with adults whose children have grown and moved away, and it's different again from what has to happen for single midlife adults who feel that faith communities have nothing to offer them.

It is evident to me that the recognition of the centrality of evangelization to the nature and identity of the church has significant implications for our lives together as Christians and as adults. These implications become clearer still as we turn to discuss the "new evangelization."

New Evangelization

The themes that run through the documents on evangelization serve as the foundation for our exploration of the "new evangelization." Like evangelization in general, the new evangelization is a multifaceted reality that is essential to the nature of the church and is the responsibility of all its members. In many ways, the defining characteristic of the new evangelization is its awareness of, and responsiveness to, the cultural setting in which it takes place.

The central focus is set out in the "Message to the People of God"[9] prepared by the bishops of the synod on the new evangelization in 2012. Citing Pope Benedict XVI, the document states that "it is an evangelization that is directed 'principally at those who, though baptized, have drifted away from the Church and live without reference to the Christian life...'"(2). To address this focus, it is imperative to give attention to two different but complementary components. On the one hand, there is a need to reach out to those who have left the church for any of a variety of reasons. There is a need for openness, dialogue, and reconciliation. On the other hand, at the same time and also very important, there is the need to reinvigorate and renew the life of the church itself. The parish, as local embodiment of the church in a given context, must be open to others, willing to engage in conversation, and hospitable. We must honestly and consistently ask ourselves: what is the nature of the parish to which we are welcoming people back?

In addition to naming the focus of the new evangelization, the "Message to the People of God" also describes the way in which this evangelization is new: "The changed social, cultural, economic, civil, and religious scenarios call us to something new: to live our communitarian experience of faith in a renewed way and to proclaim it through an evangelization that is '*new in its ardor, in its methods, in its expressions*', as John Paul II said" (2). Examining these three dimensions that are new can cast light on the work of the new evangelization.

NEW IN ITS ARDOR. Two complementary sources for this new zeal and enthusiasm can be traced out from the discussions at the synod and from the "Message to the People of God." At the heart of all evangelization is the call for those engaged to root their ministry in their relationship to Jesus Christ. In writing about the new evangelization, this theme is emphasized repeatedly. One's relationship with Jesus is the energizing source for evangelization; renewing and strengthening that relationship is the foundation for the new evangelization. At the same time, there is a repeated call to reinvigorate the life of the Christian community. Our parishes must be welcoming places where active disciples effectively engage in the work of proclaiming and witnessing to God's presence in their lives and the life of the community. This "new ardor" comes from each person's intimate relationship with Jesus and from the renewal of parish life.

NEW IN ITS METHODS. In the earlier discussion, there was the recognition that evangelization is made up of a variety of modes—witness and proclamation, inner conversion and social transformation, for example. The call for a new evangelization requires us to rethink how we engage in these various activities, always asking what it means to bring the Good News into these times and contexts. We do this by employing new expressions.

NEW IN ITS EXPRESSIONS. To speak of the expressions of the new evangelization is to ask about the vehicles through which it takes place. One of the primary expressions that deserve attention in our work of evangelization is the means of social communication. "Message to the People of God" states it clearly: "Evangelization requires that we pay much attention to the world of social communication, especially the new media, in which many lives, questions and expectations converge" (10). With an emphasis on a new evangelization, the parish is challenged to go beyond a static parish website where the only thing that changes is the weekly bulletin. Drawing on the people in the parish who have expertise with social media—including Facebook, Twitter, Pinterest, etc.—would be an important element of new evangelization.

In addition, various lay ecclesial movements play an important role in evangelization. "With regard to the laity, a special word goes to the various forms of old and new associations, together with the ecclesial movements and the new communities: All are an expression of the richness of the gifts that the Spirit bestows on the Church" (MPG 8). These are recognized as a source of evangelization, a force for renewal of the parish, and a place of welcome to those who might be returning.

Finally, when we speak about new expressions of evangelization, we also make mention of those opportunities for informal conversation about issues of faith that are particularly addressed to young adults. "Theology on Tap" and the college-campus version, "Agape Latte," are good examples of how it is possible to address the changing social and cultural context within which young adults live and make meaning of their lives.

The final document to consider in our discussion of the new evangelization is the apostolic exhortation by Pope Francis, *Evangelii Gaudium* (2013).[10] The opening paragraph sets the tone for the whole document.

> The joy of the gospel fills the hearts and lives of all who en-
> counter Jesus. Those who accept his offer of salvation are
> set free from sin, sorrow, inner emptiness, and loneliness.
> With Christ joy is constantly born anew. In this Exhortation
> I wish to encourage the Christian faithful to embark upon
> a new chapter of evangelization marked by this joy, while
> pointing out new paths for the Church's journey in years to
> come. [EG 1]

It is the joy of the gospel expressed in the lives of believers that is the foundation for an evangelization that transforms the church and the world around it. The exhortation continues by exploring a series of issues that relate to the church's capacity to be an evange-lizing agent: "the reform of the Church in her missionary outreach; the temptations faced by pastoral workers; the Church, under-stood as the entire People of God which evangelizes; the homily and its preparation; the inclusion of the poor in society; peace and dialogue within society; the spiritual motivations for mission" (EG 17). In the examination of each of these topics, Pope Francis sets out the essential dimensions of church life that contribute to ef-fective evangelization marked by enthusiasm and vitality.

Evangelization in all its forms is a challenge to the church to-day, and it requires our best efforts and significant investment of time, energy, and resources. And central to that endeavor is a well-formed community of adults; we turn to that in the next section.

Questions for reflection and conversation

★ *How has this discussion enhanced, deepened, confirmed, or challenged your understanding of evangelization?*

★ *Many of the documents affirm that the work of evangelization is the responsibility of all the members of the church. What difference does that make to how you think about your involvement in the life of the parish? How you think about decisions you make in your day-to-day life?*

★ *In what ways is your faith community an effective agent of evangelization? In what areas might it need renewal or revitalization?*

Adult Catechesis for Evangelization

At the same time that the ecclesial documents concerning evangelization were being published and beginning to shape the way theologians and pastoral leaders thought about the life of the church, a series of documents on catechesis was being promulgated. One of the earliest of these, the General Catechetical Directory (GCD, 1971),[11] included a quote that would, in part or in whole, appear in catechetical documents for the next forty years:

> Catechesis for adults, since it deals with persons who are capable of an adherence that is fully responsible, must be

considered the chief form of catechesis. All the other forms, which are indeed always necessary, are in some way oriented to it. **[20]**

So we have been saying in our official church documents for over forty years that the chief form of catechesis is the catechesis of adults. It doesn't seem inappropriate to ask, "What happened?" Or better, "What *didn't* happen?"

It is possible to propose valid and good reasons why that vision of the primary form of catechesis did not come to fruition. The first is the high emphasis we place on our responsibility to provide a context within which the next generation can grow in their faith. The structuring of most of our parishes is built around the catechesis of children and youth. Even if there is no Catholic school connected with the parish, significant investment of time, energy, and resources is most often directed toward the young. The primary focus of publishers is on programs for children and youth; if there is something for adults or families, it is in the context of the children's program, often as an add-on. Often those who have responsibility for religious education within a parish are trained and have experience with programs for children; those with experience and expertise facilitating adult learning are few. Taken together, these dynamics have often worked against real attention being given to the catechesis of adults.

But I propose that a major reason we have not yet implemented the vision that the chief form of catechesis involves adults is that we really didn't know why that was the case, *why the catechesis of adults was so crucial.* Those of us who have been working in the field of religious education or adult faith formation might well recognize the evolution of our approach to adult catechesis. Hearing the call to make catechesis of adults the chief form of catechesis, we began to think about what programs we could offer. So we established Bible studies or lecture series or special programs during Advent and Lent. These were often fairly uncoordinated, with each event or program standing (or falling) on its own. And fall many of them did. We would offer what we thought would be interesting topics, but "they" wouldn't come. I remember as a DRE myself in the late 1970s offering a great video series on the history of the church and seldom getting anyone to show up beyond the planning committee, who, I think, felt they had to be there. But if someone was to ask us why we were offering these programs for adults, our responses would tend to be fairly vague: to offer something for adults, to teach them about their faith, to help them grow in their faith. If pushed and asked why that was important, we might be somewhat stumped for an answer. I think the answer of why adult faith formation is the chief form of catechesis rests in our commitment to evangelization.

A document from the International Council for Catechesis,[12] "Adult Catechesis in the Christian Community," spells out the relationship between evangelization and adult faith formation most clearly:

> In summary, in order for the Good News of the Kingdom
> to penetrate all the various layers of the human family, it is
> crucial that every Christian play an active part in the coming
> of the Kingdom...All of this naturally requires adults to play
> a primary role. Hence it is not only legitimate, but necessary
> to acknowledge that a fully Christian community can only
> exist when a systematic catechesis of all its members takes

place and when an effective and well-developed catechesis
of adults is regarded as the *central task* in the catechetical
enterprise. [25]

In order for effective evangelization to take place, everyone must
be involved and adults need to play a primary role. For a parish to
be what a Christian community is called to be—an evangelizing
agent—requires that adults be prepared for the task. Therefore,
the faith formation of adults is to be seen as the "*central task* in
the catechetical enterprise."

To situate the faith formation of adults within the context
of evangelization, to see it as essential to an evangelizing community, is to change the primary question we ask when we think
about parish catechesis in general and adult catechesis in particular. Within the prior framework, the primary question we
ask most often centers on children and what the children are
learning or experiencing. In that case, when it comes to adults we
ask, "What do the adults need to know or learn in order to teach
or support the children in their faith development?" When we
see adult faith as inextricably connected to evangelization, the
question changes. Now the primary question attends to what the
adult community needs to talk about or experience in order that
they can most effectively be about "bringing the Good News into
all the strata of humanity, and through its influence transforming
humanity from within and making it new" (EN 18).

Let me give you an example: sacramental preparation programs for parents. Designed for parents whose children are
preparing for first celebrations of reconciliation and Eucharist,
these have consisted of anywhere from two to ten sessions that
run throughout the school year. As I reflect back on my own ex-

perience of teaching or facilitating these types of programs for a number of years, I think it is possible to trace a movement in the focus of the programs. At first, the primary theme of these sessions focused on what the children were learning, when they needed to be at practices, and what they needed to wear for First Communion. Over time these evolved to focus on the adult version of what the children were learning, sometimes integrating discussion questions to complement the presentation. What I am proposing here is that taking evangelization and the role of adults in that process seriously requires that we change the focus. Where, in the past, the dominant question was "What are the children learning?" now I think the question is "What do adults need to be talking about in order to recognize and to be signs of God's presence (sacrament) to their families and to the world?"

So the point of adult catechesis is not simply to make more knowledgeable Catholics. Its goal is to support adults in their move toward mature faith and in developing their capacity to be evangelizing agents in the world. We look at this more closely in the next chapter when we examine the characteristics that mark mature faith and the approaches we might use in supporting adults in their faith journey.

Questions for Reflection and Conversation

★ *What difference does it make to your understanding of adult faith formation to say that it is meant to prepare adults for their role as evangelizers?*

★ *Have you experienced opportunities for adult faith formation that you think have prepared you to be an evangelizer? In what ways?*

★ *What steps might your own faith community take to make adult faith formation more connected to the work of evangelization?*

Keep in Mind

• The description of evangelization that we find in *Evangelii Nuntiandi* is a helpful place to begin our discussions here: "bringing the Good News into all the strata of humanity, and through its influence transforming humanity from within and making it new" (18).

• Church documents are our friends. This is particularly true of those documents that address catechesis and evangelization; they serve as helpful beginning points for how we understand and address these important ministries.

• Bringing the themes of the church documents on evangelization together, we can say four things about evangelization: it is at the heart of what it means to be church; it is the primary responsibility of the church and all its members; it is multifaceted and complex; it is reflective of the cultural and religious situation of those being evangelized.

• "New evangelization" refers to that aspect of evangelization that gives particular attention to those who, though baptized, have little connection with the church or relationship to Christ's teachings.

• This new evangelization—new in its ardor, methods, and expressions—focuses both on inviting those who have been baptized back into relationship with the church and on making the parish an inviting, hospitable, and open place in which to welcome them.

• There is an essential link between the call to evangelization and the necessity of adult faith formation: at the heart of adult catechesis is the commitment to be and become ever more effective agents of evangelization.

CHAPTER THREE

Forming Adult Faith

HOW DO ADULTS GROW IN THEIR FAITH? HOW DO ADULTS both gain more knowledge and insight about the faith and deepen their relationship with God? Clearer questions might be: How have *you* grown in your faith? What have been the experiences that have enhanced your knowledge and insight about the faith and deepened your relationship with God?

Here are the ways three people responded to those questions.

In her mid-forties, Maryanne is the single parent of two teenagers; with work and family, her life is pretty busy. But when she stopped long enough to respond to those questions, this is what she said:

> About a year and a half ago, a friend invited me to go on a weekend retreat at a center run by some religious community. The topic was "Finding God in a Busy Life." My first reaction was, how was I ever going to get away for a weekend. But arrangements fell into place—the kids stayed overnight at friends' homes and I was able to get off work early on Friday.

I don't know what I was expecting from the retreat, but it certainly was a great experience and significant to my faith. The way the person giving the retreat talked about having a relationship with God was all new to me. I'd just never thought of that. I mean, the kids and I went to Mass most Sundays and I would sometimes pray for things or for other people, and I would sometimes even thank God when something worked out well or when there was a beautiful sunset. But I never thought about a relationship with God... or that God would want to have one with me. Throughout the retreat we looked at gospel passages about how Jesus took time from his busy life for prayer in order to foster his relationship with God.

I can't say the retreat changed my life, though in some ways it kind of did. My relationship with Jesus has been made stronger. Most mornings I begin my day by reading a brief Scripture verse and a reflection from a book of daily reflections I got on retreat. I also joined the parish book club where we read books on spirituality, which I find really helpful. I'm not perfect, but I know my relationship with Jesus has changed and grown because of that retreat.

Robert is a lector in his parish and teaches fifth grade in the parish religious education program. For him, working with the fifth graders has had a significant effect on his faith.

This is my third year teaching fifth-grade religious ed, and I would have to say that it has really helped my faith to grow. Working with the fifth graders with the focus on the church and sacraments has really helped me come to a better understanding of and appreciation for the Christian community.

40

The book we use with the kids has lots of good background material for the teachers—I found much of that really interesting and informative. I've spread out from there and read a couple of books on the church today; I'm thinking about taking an online course that looks at the sacraments.

Particularly helpful is the small group of catechists that I meet with once a month. We gather for prayer and to discuss the next month's theme and sessions, connecting when we can to the liturgical year. It always strengthens my faith to see the faith of the other catechists at work.

One of the places where I really see a difference is in my connection with the faith community. I see the importance of my involvement and commitment to the church and the ways I can live out my membership. I think it helps me grow in my relationship with God and the church.

And finally, Bob and Margie respond to the question of how have they grown in their faith by talking about their involvement in the parish social justice committee. Margie tells it this way:

Once our kids graduated from high school and then finished college and went off on our own, Bob and I kind of lost a sense of connection with the church. We went to Mass every Sunday, but there didn't seem to be much being offered that interested us. We really aren't joiners, and the bit we do as eucharistic ministers and lectors just didn't really connect us very well with the life of the parish. Then Katrina hit.

Now, we don't live anywhere near New Orleans, but for some reason the devastation and loss from that hurricane just really got to us. We did what we usually do in the face of disaster—we sent money through the Red Cross and other reputable agencies. But that didn't seem to be enough. Then Bob spotted a piece in the parish bulletin inviting anyone interested in supporting the people affected by Katrina to a meeting. We went to that meeting, and I would have to say that our lives and our faith haven't been the same since.

Two things: first, we got really involved in service; we even ended up going down there to help with rebuilding a community center that had been destroyed by the floods. When we got back, we joined others in talking at Mass one Sunday about our experience. Second was what we learned about Catholic social teaching. I'm not even sure either of us knew what that was before this. Tom, one of the people involved in the Katrina project, teaches theology at the local Catholic high school. He gave a presentation one night about the basics of Catholic social teaching and gave us some articles and things to read about it. I was really impressed; it made me proud to be a Catholic knowing that the church has been teaching so clearly on these matters.

Yes, I would say definitely that our involvement with Katrina and other things the social justice committee has been doing have really strengthened my faith, helped my faith to grow.

Three different people with very different stories of how their own faith has been enhanced and strengthened. They each point to a distinctive way in which their understanding of faith and its place in their lives was changed and supported. What about you? As we look more closely at the nature of catechesis within the context of evangelization, take a few minutes to name for yourself: how have you grown in your faith? What have been the experiences that have enhanced your knowledge and insight about the faith and deepened your relationship with God?

In this chapter, the focus is on catechesis, particularly adult catechesis, and its place in the life of the church. We begin by delineating some terms—evangelization, catechesis, and faith formation—and describing their interrelationship. Then, after briefly talking about the characteristics of mature adult faith, we look at fundamental goals of adult catechesis and discuss some of the practices and skills that relate to them. Examining these goals provides a point of departure for a parish's conversation about the nature and expression of adult faith formation.

What's the Bottom Line?

As soon as we set evangelization as the fundamental work of the church and the reason for the church's existence,[1] we gain clarity as to the central place of catechesis in the life of the church. *Catechesi Tradendae* expresses it this way:

> evangelization...is a rich, complex, and dynamic reality, made
> up of elements, or one could say moments, that are essential
> and different from each other, and that must all be kept in
> view simultaneously. Catechesis is one of these moments—a
> very remarkable one—in the whole process of evangeliza-
> tion. [18]

As a moment of evangelization, catechesis shares in many of the qualities of evangelization that were examined in the last chapter. Like evangelization, catechesis is not simply the responsibility of select people; it is the work of the whole church and central to the church's mission. Just as the whole community and all its members are called to be engaged in the work of evangelization, the community itself is to be the context where catechesis takes place. And like evangelization, effective catechesis takes many forms and expressions, responding with care to the social and cultural context of the participants.

Catechesis can only be understood when situated within the context of evangelization. Evangelization is the fundamental reason for the church's existence; catechesis is an essential moment in that enterprise. That means that anything we do in catechesis and, really, in any ministry of the word must have as its aim preparing people for the task of evangelization.

Evangelization begins with *Christian witness*, the lived example of those whose lives have been shaped by the gospel. The *initial proclamation* is the response a person gives when asked for the reason for their hope (1 Peter 3:15). Through the work of the Holy Spirit, this initial proclamation leads to initial conversion and, in light of that, opens the person up to *initiatory catechesis* leading to baptism.

As the GDC makes clear, initiatory catechesis is to be comprehensive and systematic; it cannot be simply periodical or occasional. The document goes on to say, "Being essential, it looks to what is 'common' for the Christian, without entering into disputed questions nor transforming itself into a form of theological investigation" (68). In many ways, initiatory catechesis is modeled on the catechumenate; "it is an apprenticeship of the entire Christian life," which means that it goes beyond simply instruction to include integration into the life of the community, participation in liturgy, and introduction to the mission of the church.

But catechesis for adults goes beyond initiatory catechesis. As adults mature in their faith, *continuing catechesis* is needed to further their conversion to Christ. Here is where in-depth study of Scripture and a deepening of the Christian message through theological instruction can take place. This form of catechesis may be more occasional, rooted in particular times of life and key human experiences. But like all the pastoral activities of the parish, this ongoing or continuing catechesis has the task of preparing adults to be and become ever more effective evangelizers.

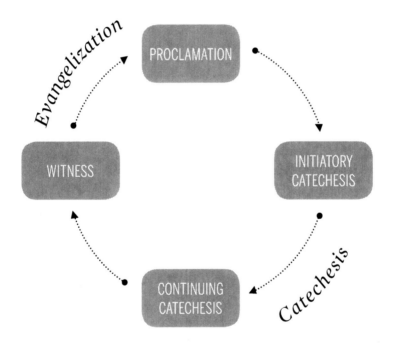

One more phrase that needs describing in this context: adult faith formation. Seeing this as very much a part of and in service to evangelization, I am using the term faith formation to refer to the wide variety of ways in which adults grow in their faith. In this context, it includes both initiatory and continuing catechesis (intentional, structured instruction/formation); liturgy, community, and service (the forms through which the church expresses itself[2]); and other informal ways in which the faith of adults is enhanced.

In all of this, the bottom line is evangelization. Through evangelization, we receive the first proclamation of the Good News of Jesus Christ and become open to God's word. That initial conversion is nurtured through initiatory catechesis and further enhanced through continuing catechesis. This is complemented by other modes of faith formation. But the relationship between evangelization and faith formation does not end there. This in turn forms adults to be an evangelizing people with mature faith, living lives that give witness to the power of the gospel in their lives.

Fostering Adult Faith

How do we describe mature adult faith, the kind of faith that supports someone in living life as a person of faith able to witness to the power of the gospel in his or her life? *Our Hearts Were Burning Within Us* (OHWB),[3] a document specifically addressing adult faith formation, published by the United States Conference of Catholic Bishops in 1999, characterizes adult faith as "living, explicit, and fruitful."[4] By *living*, the writers of the document mean that it is a dynamic response to God's invitation to relationship. Because it is living, it shares the characteristics of living things: "it grows and develops over time; it learns from experience; it adapts to changing conditions while maintaining its essential identity; it goes through seasons, some apparently dormant, others fruitful, though wherever faith is present the Holy Spirit is at work in the life of the disciple" (OHWB 50). It also needs to be nurtured in a supportive and vibrant environment. Mature faith is *explicit* in that it is "explicitly rooted in a personal relationship with Jesus lived in the Christian community" (55). In addition, it explicitly connects to the teachings and mission of the church. And finally, mature faith is *fruitful*. In other words, it is a faith that is put into action, that makes a difference in how a person lives his or her life. Here the document points to the fruits of the Spirit as listed in Galatians 5, the fruits of compassion and justice and the fruit of evangelization as important points of reference in describing fruitful faith.

Living, explicit, fruitful: these are rich descriptors of mature faith and a good starting point to keep in mind as we think about how we foster that kind of faith. Following its discussion of these three dimensions of mature faith, OHWB then sets out three goals for adult faith formation: invite and enable ongoing conversion to Jesus in holiness of life, promote and support active membership in the Christian community, and call and prepare adults to act as disciples in mission to the world. These goals are designed to guide us in how we think about the ways in which mature adult faith is supported.

1. Invite and enable ongoing conversion to Jesus in holiness of life
At the heart of all catechesis is the person of Jesus and our relationship with him. *Catechesi Tradendae* states that "the definitive aim of catechesis is to put people not only in touch but in communion, in intimacy, with Jesus Christ" (5).[5] Catechesis is the invitation to strengthen one's bond with Jesus that is established at baptism, deepened through confirmation, and celebrated in the Eucharist. Through catechesis we enter into an apprenticeship to the whole of the Christian life, with Jesus Christ at the center (GDC 63).

How do we "invite and enable ongoing conversion to Jesus

in holiness of life"? Or to ask that question another way: what skills or practices need to be fostered in order to enable adults to enter more deeply into their relationship with Jesus? As the story of Maryanne at the beginning of this chapter points out, a relationship with Jesus is a central aspect of how we mature in our faith, and two of the primary ways of fostering that relationship are engaging Scripture, particularly the gospels, and establishing patterns of personal prayer. Each of these serves as the foundation of our relationship with Jesus and can be integrated into multiple modes of adult formation in a variety of ways.

When we think about enhancing the capacity of adults to engage Scripture, our thoughts first turn to Bible study. And this can be an important component of the structured programs that a parish offers the adult community. This can include planning and facilitating small group Bible study,[6] encouraging participation in online Scripture study opportunities,[7] and providing recommendations for those interested in daily personal Scripture reflection.[8] In addition, integrating engagement with Scripture, particularly the Sunday gospel reading, into all the settings where adults gather is an effective way to assist adults to prayerfully engage the Scriptures. An adapted and simplified *lectio divina* provides a helpful model.[9]

The process begins with a slow and attentive reading of the text (*lectio*), simply listening to the reading and noticing what stands out to you from the text. This is followed by a time for reflecting on the text and its meaning (*meditatio*); what is this text saying to you and your life experience? This would also be an opportunity for people to share with one another or with the group the insight that they are getting from the text. The third movement involves allowing the text to speak to you; this could include silently repeating a particular word or phrase from the text (*contemplatio*). And finally, what would you say to God in response to this reading? What prayer does this reading elicit from you (*oratio*)? This could be done effectively in as little as ten minutes at the beginning of a meeting or as the opening of a catechetical session.

There are three key benefits to introducing reflection on the Sunday gospel to your meetings and gatherings of adults. First, by engaging in this practice regularly, adults become comfortable with reflecting on the Scriptures in light of their own experience. Asking what verses seemed particularly pertinent to them models for adults the importance of reading Scripture in terms of their lives. Second, by encouraging adults to share their reflections, whether in pairs, small groups, or the full gathering, they grow in their competency to talk about Scripture and to share their faith with others. Finally, there is a benefit to the whole community. Reflecting on Sunday's gospel at all parish gatherings means that the entire community is reflecting on a common theme and making that theme relevant to their lives in a way that connects all to the primary gathering of the parish, the Sunday assembly.

In addition to encouraging adults to engage with the Scriptures, catechesis also enhances their relationship with Jesus through fostering commitment to personal prayer. The Catholic tradition is rich in resources around this aspect of Christian life. Centering prayer, the Jesus prayer, the *examen*, the rosary as well as modes of meditation and contemplation: all these serve to enhance one's relationship with Jesus. Of importance here is assisting adults to recognize the close connection between personal prayer and lived Christian faith; our capacity to live effectively as Christians in the world and to be evangelizers depends on personal prayer.

2. Promote and support active membership in the Christian community

While it is paramount to adult faith that persons enhance their relationship with Jesus Christ, this most effectively takes place within the context of a mature Christian community whose own faith is living, explicit, and fruitful. As we saw in the opening story of Robert, there are a variety of ways in which to promote and support active engagement with the faith community. Two that I want to discuss here focus on supporting adults to recognize the central role of liturgy and on providing a context in which they can understand the balance between memory and openness in the church's identity. By enriching adults' understanding of these two elements, we provide a context within which people can deepen their commitment in the community of faith.

For Catholics, the center of our community life is the liturgy, particularly the Eucharist; we have heard repeatedly that it is the "source and summit of the Christian life" (*Lumen Gentium* 11; CCC 1324). All the other sacraments, and indeed all the pastoral activities of the parish, flow from the Eucharist. As the effective sign of the paschal mystery—the remembrance of the death and resurrection of Jesus as source of our redemption—the Eucharist is the primary celebration of the core of Christian belief and the foundation of Christian life.

And yet the reality is that on any given Sunday about 30% of Catholics attend Mass.[10] There are myriad dynamics to explain the low attendance; no one reason—lousy liturgies or homilies, busy lives, sexual abuse scandal, rise of secularism, etc.—suffices. The point here is not to launch into a harangue about people not attending Mass; it is simply to remember that even those who may be participating in some other element of parish life—

programs for parents of children receiving first sacraments, for example—may not be participating in the Sunday assembly. But this should not keep us from investing efforts in establishing the centrality of the Eucharist.

The primary way we support participation in liturgy is by having good liturgies. Often, the more people who are engaged in planning, implementing, and evaluating the liturgies, the better.[11] By taking the time to set out the criteria by which a Sunday liturgy is evaluated and then applying those criteria to liturgies on a regular basis, we enhance the possibility of having effective liturgies for the community. It is also helpful to have a vibrant, active liturgy committee that sees that its role includes, among other things, listening to what people have to say about Sunday liturgy in all the informal places that people meet.[12]

In addition to good liturgy, it is important to be intentional about placing the liturgy at the center of the parish's life. Using the Sunday gospel as the focus of opening prayer for all the committees and groups that gather in a parish during a week is one way to connect people back to the commonly shared Sunday assembly. When more extensive prayer is used for an event, the music used on Sunday can also be a reminder of the community's celebration. When appropriate, the liturgy or the time after liturgy can be used as an opportunity to acquaint the community with elements of parish life that take place outside of Sunday Mass. I am thinking, for example, of having participants in "mission trips" speak at the end of Mass about their experiences, or having the names of candidates for RCIA, people on the parish council, first communicants, and confirmandi displayed at the entrance of the church at various times. Weaving elements of the liturgy into the week's activities, and the week's activities into the liturgy, is one way to make the connection with liturgy central to the life of the parish, which supports participation.

The second element I am proposing here as important to the task of promoting active membership in the Christian community is fostering a sense of the balance between memory and openness.[13] How do we sort out some of the key tensions in the life of the parish or of the church at large? How do we understand those who differ with us? How do we welcome them and their ideas with a genuine sense of hospitality? One way to grapple with these questions is by understanding the creative tension between memory and openness.

If I were to ask a group of people, "What is the most important dimension of being Catholic?" the responses would be as numerous and varied as the number of people present. Some people feel that it is the traditions of the church that are most important and meaningful to them. Perhaps it is the familiar rhythm of the Sunday liturgy or the place of devotions to Mary. The consistency of the church's prayer and ritual over the years and the clarity of Catholic teaching: these traditions are important for them. Others, however, find their reasons for being Catholic connected with the church's vision of the future as reflected in the writings of Vatican Council II that challenged the church to "read the signs of the times." The church looks to the future when it works to overcome the effects of oppression or when it strives to address the social and ethical issues facing people today. Remembering the traditions of the past or being open to the future: people can easily disagree on what is more important to our Catholic faith, and these different points of view can often lead to tension within the church, and within a parish community. But there is good news within our Catholic tradition—both a respect for the past and an eye on the future are key elements in what it means to live our lives as Catholics. We can understand these elements as "memory" and "openness." By "memory," we refer to all those elements that make up our Catholic tradition. By "openness," we mean taking into account the experience and insights of believers today.[14]

We are a church rooted in a long and solid tradition. Paul's letter to the Ephesians makes that clear when it says that we are part of the household of God "built upon the foundation of the apostles and prophets, with Christ Jesus himself being the capstone" (Ephesians 2:20). We are a people rooted in the firm foundation of the past, a people who value and depend upon *memory*. At the same time, the church exists not as a past, complete reality, but as a living, breathing entity located in a specific time and place. Paul writes just a verse or so later in his letter to the Ephesians, "in [the Lord] you also are being built together into a dwelling place of God in the Spirit" (Ephesians 2:22). In addition to a people who value and depend upon memory, we are also a people drawn to the future, guided by the Holy Spirit with a lively sense of *openness*.

The history of the church is marked by times of tensions that can be traced back to a disagreement over the balance between memory and openness. As early as the Acts of the Apostles we see a conflict between Paul and some of the Jewish leaders over whether Gentiles needed to follow Jewish laws in order to be Christian. Some of the Jewish leaders argued from the perspective of memory: we have always done it this way. The earliest Christians were Jewish; Jesus was Jewish. Paul, however, argues from the perspective of openness; he believed that he was called to preach to the Gentiles and bring the good news that they are saved through Jesus. This issue was debated at length and was finally decided in favor of Paul at the Council of Jerusalem about the year 50 CE. Our history is shaped by how the tension between memory and openness is negotiated, sometimes favoring one and sometimes the other. Some of our saints came to prominence as they tried to return the church to a more balanced sense of the relationship between memory and openness.

How can a sense of balance between memory and openness enhance active participation in the Christian community? First, by giving us a helpful way to talk about the difference within a parish community and within the larger church. At times it seems easy to dismiss someone's perspective as "too conservative" or "too liberal." An understanding of memory and openness allows us to reframe the conversation in terms of what people value and cherish about the church. Second, it makes clear that we all *need* the Christian community: whether we tend to emphasize memory or openness, it is important to recognize that no one person, no one group, has the whole picture of what it means to be Catholic. While each of us brings our own angle to the realities of the present church, our acknowledging and affirming the need for complementary and even conflicting points of view is key to what it means to be Catholic and to contributing to the ongoing vibrancy of the church. And, finally, as we look to the future of the church, whether from the perspective of memory or openness, it is important that we foster in ourselves and in future generations a willingness to engage in conversation with those whose perspectives differ from ours. As we look back at our history as a church, both recent and distant, we can see that the church has been most vital and most influential when the diverse and sometimes divergent voices have been heard.

3. Prepare adults to act as disciples in mission to the world

Not surprisingly, we return again to ideas connected with evangelization, which has as its point of entry the place where the church meets the world. As we have seen already, evangelization is multifaceted—witness and proclamation, word and sacrament, interior change and social transformation. All of these are at the heart of the task of the disciple in mission to the world. It is not sufficient for us to gather as a faith community; while that is important, we must keep ever before us the fact that we have been gathered to be sent, to be evangelizing agents in the world.

The whole work of catechesis prepares adults to act as disciples in the world. Fostering a relationship with Jesus and active participation in the faith community are essential fundamentals. Beyond that, let me mention two other elements that are essential to an adult acting as a disciple in the world: understanding and acceptance of one's baptismal rights and responsibilities, and comprehension of and ability to apply Catholic social teaching.

Lumen Gentium, one of the core documents on the church from Vatican II, has as one of its chief themes the centrality of baptism and the role that flows from initiation: acting as disciples in the world. "The faithful who by baptism are incorporated into Christ, are placed in the People of God, and in their own way share the priestly, prophetic, and kingly office of Christ, and to the best of their ability carry on the mission of the whole Christian people in the Church and in the world" (LG 31). Examining these three callings—to be a priestly people, a prophetic people, and a kingly people—can give us insight into who we are called to be by virtue of our baptism.

A priestly people—In the Old Testament, the priest was one who mediated between God and human beings and offered prayer and sacrifice on the people's behalf. In the New Testament, we hear that Jesus is the great high priest, mediating God's presence to us and offering the sacrifice of his own life for the forgiveness of sins.[15] Through our baptism we share in this priestly office by mediating God's presence through the example of our lives, by praying for and with others, and by offering our own lives in service to the reign of God.

A prophetic people—The prophet is one who speaks God's word, more often than not in opposition to the direction in which the people are moving. The words of the prophet can be words of challenge as well as words of comfort. As a prophetic people we are called to speak God's word in our own context. Attuned to the social, political, and cultural realities around us, we retell the story of God's saving action in the past and remind ourselves and others of God's lasting promises of the future.

A kingly or political people—The king is one who governs and protects; he establishes laws and structures that are at service to the people. Since the term king can be narrowly conceived and is not gender inclusive, rather than the term kingly people we can speak here of "political people," that is, people engaged and interested in the polity.[16] As a political people, we look to the structures by which decisions are made, and we work to assure their correlation with the reign of God.

These three descriptors—priestly, prophetic, and political—characterize who we are by virtue of our baptism and what it means to be disciples in service to the world. While we distinguish the three roles for the sake of analysis, in our daily living out of our baptism they are intertwined. For example: when we facilitate an RCIA group, we are acting on our priestly and prophetic roles; when we guide our children to understand right from wrong, we are acting on our prophetic and political roles; when we pray for our governmental leaders, we are engaging in our priestly and political roles. As we live out our lives as disciples in service to the world, all three of these roles are integrated in a variety of ways.

Following from our baptism is the call to act for justice in our personal relationships, our civic involvement, and our global responsibility. The second way we support adults in living as disciples in mission to the world is by making accessible the core tenets of Catholic social teaching and providing a forum for examining how to apply its principles to their lived reality.

Often referred to as the Catholic Church's best-kept secret, our social justice teaching rests on documents from the last 120 years issued by popes, Vatican II, bishops' synods, and national conferences of bishops. It is a rich and complex tradition ranging from *Rerum Novarum* in 1891, which focused on the rights of workers, to the latest papal or episcopal statement on war, poverty, or capital punishment. Here I examine four central themes that serve as key threads running through the documents; they are core to the discussion and enactment of the church's social teaching today.

1. **THE DIGNITY OF THE HUMAN PERSON.** At the heart of all social justice and human rights is the dignity of the human person. In describing this theme, the U.S. Catholic bishops write "that human life is sacred and that the dignity of the human person is the foundation of a moral vision for society. Our belief in the sanctity of human life and the inherent dignity of the human person is the foundation of all the principles of our social teaching."[17] It is our responsibility to defend the dignity of all human life. When

reflecting on the needs of the world in this area of human rights, the writers of the *General Directory for Catechesis* write: "The evangelizing activity of the Church in this field of human rights has, as its undeniable objective, the task of revealing the inviolable dignity of every human person. In a certain sense, 'it is the central and unifying task of service which the Church, and the lay faithful in her, are called to render to the human family.' Catechesis must prepare them for this task" (19).

2. PREFERENTIAL OPTION FOR THE POOR AND VULNERABLE. The moral fiber of a community or society can be evaluated by how it cares for the least privileged and the most vulnerable. In a time when the split between the rich and the poor is widening here in the United States and elsewhere, attending to those among us who struggle to address basic human needs—nutritious food, affordable housing, sustaining work—is important. As the U.S. bishops write in their 1986 pastoral letter, *Economic Justice for All*, "the obligation to provide justice for all means that the poor have the single most urgent economic claim on the conscience of the nation" (86).[18]

3. SOLIDARITY. Our responsibility to attend to issues of peace and justice extends far beyond the borders of our faith community and country. By virtue of our common humanity and the dignity we share, we are called to attend to the situation of others round the globe. This is both an economic issue and a political one. It is essential that we be aware of the way in which our habits of obtaining and consuming have an impact on those on the other side of the globe. Recognizing the fact of a common global economy means acknowledging that our decisions of how to spend our money have human rights implications in other parts of the world. At the same time, war is one of the most devastating forces against human rights and dignity. As a nation, we have a responsibility to do everything we can to avoid war and to work for a just and lasting peace in all contexts. As individuals, we have the responsibility to be engaged in our political system in such a way as to support the movement toward peace.

4. CARE FOR CREATION. A fairly recently developed theme in Catholic social teaching has focused on our responsibility for creation and the environment. In his encyclical *Caritas in Veritate,* Pope Benedict XVI wrote: "The environment is God's gift to everyone, and in our use of it we have a responsibility towards the poor, towards future generations, and towards humanity as a whole." So our care for creation is driven both by a concern for the created order itself, which is a gift from God, and by recognizing the negative impact that lack of care for the environment has on human beings, often the poor and most vulnerable.

Catholic social teaching incorporates a dual call: to serve those in need and to challenge structures that diminish the rights and dignity of human beings. These are two complementary activities, acts of charity and works for justice. It is important that both be integrated in the way in which a faith community reflects on Catholic social teaching and the way in which it is put into action. Both are part of the same fundamental call to be disciples in service to the world.

To promote the role of adults as disciples to the world, catechesis provides opportunity for adults to learn about and reflect on their roles within a priestly, prophetic, and political people. This begins by raising people's awareness of these roles and the way they have been and could be living them out in their lives.

Having celebrated the sacraments of initiation at the Easter Vigil, the following weeks might be a good time to reflect on baptism both in preaching and conversation, asking the question: "What does it mean to this community that we are a priestly, prophetic, and political people?"

At the same time, a familiarity with Catholic social teaching is an essential component to being disciples in service to the world. Catechesis prepares adults for this task by providing opportunities to learn and be in conversation about the core themes of Catholic social teaching and the implications for them and for their faith communities.

One final point: as we saw in the story of Bob and Margie, engagement in action for justice can be a point of entry into the life of the church and an opportunity for deepening one's relationship with God. In other words, these three elements—relationship with Jesus, affiliation with the Christian community, and commitment to the mission of the church in the world—are intimately connected and cyclical in nature. Adults can enter in at any point in the cycle and this can lead to a strengthening of the other aspects as well.

Question for Reflection and Conversation

★ *Which of the three goals of adult faith formation—relationship with Jesus, affiliation with the faith community, and participation in the mission of the church—do you see as most important? Why?*

★ *Reflecting on the various opportunities for adult faith formation in your parish setting, which of the three goals receives the most attention? What are the ways in which this goal is highlighted in your context? How might it be further enhanced?*

★ *Which of the three goals—relationship with Jesus, affiliation with the faith community, and participation in the mission of the church—do you think needs further attention in your pastoral setting? How might that be done?*

Keep in Mind

- As a moment of evangelization, catechesis shares in the same characteristics as evangelization: it is at the heart of what it means to be church; it is the primary responsibility of the church and all its members; it is multifaceted and complex; it is reflective of the cultural and religious situation of those being catechized.

- *Our Hearts Were Burning Within Us* (OHWB) characterizes adult faith as "living, explicit, and fruitful."

- This type of faith is sustained through the rich interplay of relationship with Jesus, affiliation with and commitment to the Christian community, and engagement with the mission of the church as disciples in the world.

- We support conversion to Jesus by encouraging adults to engage Scripture, particularly the gospels, and establish patterns of personal prayer.

- We promote active membership in the Christian community by helping support adults to recognize the central role of liturgy and by providing a context in which they can understand the balance between memory and openness in the church's identity.

- We enhance engagement with the church's mission by encouraging adults to understand and accept their baptismal rights and responsibilities, and to comprehend and apply Catholic social teaching.

Further discussion on the modes of adult catechesis are examined in the next two chapters where we look at intentional catechesis and the role of conversation in chapter four and the formative role of community life in chapter five.

CHAPTER FOUR

Adults Engaged in Conversations that Matter

ONE AFTERNOON AS I WAS DRIVING MY THEN-SEVEN-YEAR-old daughter to an appointment, we were stopped at a light to allow a funeral procession to pass. As the hearse went by, Natalya turned to me and asked, "What do they do with the heads?"

"What do they do with the heads," I repeated back to her, a technique I learned teaching undergraduate theology: sometimes repeating back a confusing question can elicit clarification, as it did in this case. "Yes," she said. "You always tell us they just bury the body, so what do they do with the heads?" This led to a conversation about what I believe about life after death that elicited further questions and comments from Natalya. Not a particularly momentous conversation, perhaps, but one of the many conversations that enhanced Natalya's faith and mine as well.

This conversation between Natalya and me can be seen as

part of a much larger ongoing conversation. Perhaps it includes a conversation between my mother and me when I was a child on the occasion of the death of a relative or a favorite pet. It also includes my conversations with undergrads as I talked about the church's teaching about death and how that is celebrated in our funeral liturgies. Maybe the theme came up in a conversation with friends as we struggled to make sense of the death of a child. All of these conversations fed into my ability to respond to Natalya's question with clarity and confidence; I was able to articulate my beliefs at that spontaneous moment because I had had the opportunity to talk about them in other settings. As we look at the way in which adults grow in their faith, conversation plays a significant role and is at the heart of this chapter.

In the next two chapters we examine the range of experiences that are formative of adult faith, which run the whole gamut from highly intentional (Bible study, Lenten parish program) to less explicitly intentional (committee work, teaching in religious education program) to the unintentional (encounters with nature, the awareness of one's mortality). In examining these we ask how we can enhance their effectiveness in shaping a people with living, explicit, and fruitful faith.

In this chapter we examine the intentional, structured programs designed to strengthen the faith of adults and assist them in making the essential link between their faith and their lives. The chapter begins by articulating some key characteristics of adult learning in the contemporary context. Since conversation is an essential component of adult faith formation, a discussion follows on the role of conversation and some suggestions on how it can be facilitated effectively. The chapter ends with some principles for planning and implementing adult programs.

In chapter five we turn to the less formal modes by which people's faith is fostered and enhanced. Particularly, we look at the role of the faith community and the way in which people's engagement with aspects of the community forms their faith and identity.

Adult Learning

An important part of the faith formation of adults centers around structured programs offered through places like parishes, dioceses, and retreat centers. These range from long-standing Bible studies and book clubs to a short-term series or single presentation or retreat day. They include intergenerational gatherings[1] and meetings open to the adult community as well as peer-group[2] programs. For all of these settings, attention to some basic characteristics of adult learning is important to the effectiveness of the program and to the satisfaction of the participants. Here I am just going to examine four key ones.

ADULT EXPERIENCE: Adults bring rich and varied experiences to any catechetical event. One of the defining elements—and one of the gifts—of working with adults is the richness and variety of experience they bring. Most adults come to a session having negotiated complex relationships, addressed life-changing questions, and weathered significant crises. All of these genuinely human experiences can and should be accessed in service to the learning of each individual and the whole community.

We begin with the experience of the learner for two reasons. First, we believe that God reveals the divine presence in and through our human experience. It is through our relationships with others that we experience love, wisdom, and compassion—

characteristics we associate with God. It is in the experiences of being startled by the beauty of a spring day and worn down by the seeming monotony of life that we experience the divine.[3] Second, the awareness of God's presence in these experiences can easily go unnoticed or not reflected upon unless we are invited to do so. That is one of the gifts we give adults—the opportunity to name their experiences and recognize God's presence.

But often the opportunities to draw out those experiences are lost. By way of example: a parish offered several sessions for parents whose children were preparing for first sacraments, with the expectation that at least one parent from each family would attend. And, for the most part, they did. The curriculum was well planned, building around six core themes that are present in the Mass—welcoming, forgiving, listening, celebrating, remembering, and going forth.[4] While well planned and effectively executed, each of the hour-long meetings consisted of a lecture on the topic that left no time for conversation among the adults. When asked about this arrangement and the absence of time for conversation, the catechetical leader said, "It would have been nice to have had time for you to talk with one another, but we had so much to tell you." The adults' experiences of forgiving, listening, or remembering could have added a depth to the sessions that was just not possible with a lecture. In the end, the experience and understanding of the adults' engagement with God, with their families, and with the child preparing for first sacraments were dismissed in favor of what those in leadership thought needed to be told.

MAKING CONNECTIONS: Adults learn best when there is an opportunity to discuss the implications of the session's content for their lives. In addition to bringing rich experience to the gathering, adults also hope to leave with new insights into how their faith connects with their lives. As religious educator Thomas Groome says, our goal is to bring "life to Faith and Faith to life."[5]

When my daughters were younger, I remember one evening watching the movie *The Color of Friendship* (2000), which has as its backdrop the 1970s struggle to overcome apartheid in South Africa. The movie is brought to its climax when Steve Biko, a member of the South African liberation movement, is killed by South African police. Demonstrations and protests take place around the world, including at the South African embassy in Washington, DC. As the movie progressed, I responded to my daughters' questions as best I could. Truth be told, I didn't have at my fingertips the dates and names of those involved in overcoming apartheid, but I could articulate to them some of the impact of apartheid in South Africa and the effect of prejudice and segregation in this country. And that was the important thing: to be able to articulate the link between the movie and what I believe. I could—and did—learn what I needed to know by checking the Internet; I filled the girls in on some of the details the next morning at breakfast. But the most important part of the conversations we had was my opportunity to speak with them about what I knew to be true.

The same thing is the case in adult catechesis. The most important aspect of what we do with adults is to assist them in articulating what they believe and making the link between their beliefs and how they live their lives. Planning and presenting the content of the session with this in mind and providing opportunity for adults to be in guided conversation about the implications for their lives are essential aspects of effective adult faith formation.

HOSPITABLE SPACE: Effective faith formation takes place in a just and hospitable space. "Space" in this context is used in both a literal and a metaphorical way. In a literal sense the hospitality of the place is reflected in the comfort of the surroundings and the care given to the environment. Having the room arranged with chairs in circles or at tables conveys something very different from one with chairs in rows facing a podium. In addition, the presence of works of art, plants, and candles marks this as a special place, a place set aside with care for the benefit of the participants.

Speaking metaphorically, a hospitable space is marked by a spirit of mutual trust and respect. Parker Palmer, in his book *To Know as We Are Known,* states, "Hospitality means receiving each other, our struggles, our newborn ideas with openness and care."[6] Hospitable space is a context in which listening and speaking are both seen as active and demanding elements of adult faith formation. It is a context where the line between "those in the know" and the "people in the pew" is set aside and all are seen as a people gathered together on the faith journey.

TRANSFORMATIVE LEARNING: Transformative learning is a defining characteristic of adult catechesis. All kinds of learning take place in programs for adults within the pastoral settings. Let's imagine, by way of example, a series of gatherings around the sacraments. On one level, the participants gain new information about the meaning of some of the signs of the sacraments or something about their history, for example. At a second level, their understanding of "sacraments" may be broadened. Perhaps they had a really narrow view of sacraments as seven discrete actions. The experience of the course—readings, reflection, and conversation—has opened up a new way of understanding the sacraments as explicit expressions of God's always-present action in the world.

Finally, at a third level, the experience of the course might lead the participants to gain new *perspectives*. This mode of learning involves questioning, critiquing, and when necessary, changing one's view of the world, one's sense of the "givenness" of how things are and how they work. For example, someone who tends to see the world as marked by sin and fraught with difficulties might be challenged by the readings, presentations, and conversations to look at this worldview again. The course could be part of a process by which this person creates a new meaning perspective, one that is shot through with recognition of the grace of God. This is transformative learning.

We can define transformative learning as the process by which our taken-for-granted view of the world (perspective, paradigm) is critically examined in light of new information and understandings. Through this critical examination, we begin to question the adequacy of our worldview and, as necessary, make changes. Let me give an example that I develop more fully in *Toward an Adult Church*.[7]

Jim was raised in a family where the father's role was to supply for the family's needs and solve the major problems that they may encounter. Although Jim has never articulated it, he has taken on that perspective in his relationship with his wife, Ellen, and their three sons. This worldview—though implicitly held—had functioned well enough during the early years of his growing family. There had been nothing that challenged it or called it into question. However, as his younger son, Ryan, began to move out of his toddler years, it became increasingly clear that there was a problem—he tended to stay separate from other family members, didn't play well with other children, and tended to get overly focused on a particular object or activity. (He was later diagnosed as being on the autism spectrum.) And Jim had a hard time dealing with Ryan; no matter what Jim did, he came away feeling frustrated and even angry. At some level he was attempting to do what he always did, what his worldview called him to do: solve the family's problems. But he couldn't seem to "solve" Ryan.

It was in this context that Jim went—reluctantly—to the sessions for parents of children preparing for First Eucharist; his older son, Steven, was in second grade. Jim learned quite a bit in these sessions—new information about the sacraments and new understandings of what faith means. He also gained information and understandings through which his perspective or worldview about his role as father was challenged. The most important one happened during conversation time, when one of the other fathers present talked about his son who was having difficulties in school. Jim was surprised at how freely the father talked about the challenges involved in raising a child with special needs. At one point, the father said, "It took me a long time to get over the feeling that I had to fix my son, make him or his experience of school 'all better.'"

Through his experience in these adult sessions—and many other experiences that colored his life, including his interactions with Ryan and Ellen—Jim began to think and then think *differently* about his role as father and his relationship with Ryan. Over time he changed his worldview in this arena, seeing himself and his role in his family in a more expansive, inclusive, and life-giving way.

Clearly, the DRE who planned the sessions did not have as an objective: "change the meaning perspective of participants regarding their role as parents." And the transformative learning was not completed through this one event. But conversation among the participants, with guidance from well-prepared questions and an active facilitator, certainly contributed to it. And it is to a discussion of conversation that we turn now.

Questions for Reflection and Conversation

✳ *How are these four characteristics of adult learning—experience, connection with lived faith, hospitality, and transformative learning—present in the adult formation you have experienced? How might they be further enhanced?*

✳ *Reflect on a time when your perspective on something changed significantly, a time when you questioned or examined the presupposition behind a perspective or view that you held. What do you think contributed to this experience of transformative learning?*

Conversation

Central to each of these four characteristics of adult learning—experience, hospitality, connections with lived faith, and transformative learning—is the role of conversation. Adults grow in their faith best when they have the opportunity to engage in conversation with other adults about things that matter. We can speak of four core reasons why conversation around issues of faith is essential to the ongoing development of adult faith. Each of these four outcomes of conversation serves as an important dynamic in enhancing a faith that is living, explicit, and fruitful.

71

CONVERSATION:

- *enhances our ability to express our faith.* Having the opportunity to reflect "out loud" on our faith gives us a sense of confidence in our abilities to articulate our beliefs. We find ourselves more comfortable talking about our faith with our children, family, and friends once we have had the chance, in conversation, to give expression to our ideas and beliefs.

- *gives us the opportunity to come to clarity about what we think and believe.* It is in the give-and-take of conversation that we examine more closely the beliefs and ideas that we have and the presumptions that rest behind them. A statement about what one believes generally includes presuppositions about who God is and who human beings are. It is in trying to help others understand our point of view that these presuppositions become clearer to us; we can then look at them more closely and evaluate their adequacy for our lives.

- *provides a context for seeing connection between faith and life.* It is often in conversation that we ask ourselves, or are asked by others, the most important theological question we can ask: "So what?" So what does this belief mean for how you live your life? How does that practice shape how you raise your children or treat your coworkers? In addition, hearing how other people have worked through some of the challenges of living as a Christian in a secularized context can help us to see our own way through a similar experience.

- *strengthens our faith as we hear about the faith of others.* It is renewing to hear others speak about their faith. Sometimes we are in awe of the faith that someone might show forth. Other times we identify with the doubts or struggles of someone else. In either case, our own faith is strengthened by hearing of the lived faith of those who share our conversations.

But in order for conversation to function in these ways, it must be *sustained, engaged,* and *critical.*

SUSTAINED: Conversation is most effective when it is for an adequate period of time over an extended period of time. The single five-minute discussion period at the end of an hour presentation can easily lead to frustration rather than really transformative conversation. Allowing sufficient time for conversation gives the participants the opportunity to become comfortable with the group, to think about their reactions to the questions at hand, and to begin to bring their insights into dialogue with their lived faith. One rule of thumb I try to maintain is that the time for discussion should be at least equal to the length of the presentation.

While it is important that each conversation period be of a substantive length of time, it is also helpful to have more than one period of discussion over the length of the course or workshop. I, for one, find it difficult to change my mind or even alter my position in a single conversation. I need distance from the topic, time to reflect on my ideas, and the opportunity to understand more clearly my own response. The same dynamic applies to my openness to the position of others and my ability to truly understand another person's point of view, particularly if it is significantly different from mine. Coming back around to examine the general theme again—the sacraments, catechesis, and Scripture, for example—from a somewhat different angle provides the opportunity for the give-and-take that marks effective conversation.

ENGAGED: Someone described most of our day-to-day conversations as a series of monologues that we take turns saying to one another. In the book *Truth and Method*, Hans-Georg Gadamer describes conversation as a much more engaged and engaging activity: "Conversation is a process of coming to an understanding. Thus it belongs to every true conversation that each person opens himself to the other, truly accepts his point of view as valid and transposes himself into the other to such an extent that he understands not the particular individual but what he says."[8] To be engaged in a conversation means more than simply arguing your own point; it involves actively listening to the other, giving him or her the benefit of the doubt, presuming in their favor.

In addition to active listening, being engaged in the conversation means allowing for the back-and-forthness of the conversation. David Tracy, in *The Analogical Imagination,*[9] says that engaging in conversation is risky, not just because your ideas might not be accepted or your position may be overruled. Engaged conversation is risky because you might have to change your mind!

CRITICAL: Here we return to the earlier discussion of transformative learning. At the heart of that mode of learning is the capacity to critically examine the presumptions that serve as the foundation for our making meaning of the world. Effective conversation gives us the opportunity to look and then look again at the "givens" that shape how we see the world. At times, the simple act of bringing those to articulation is sufficient to further the process of asking, "What do I think about this? Why do I think this way? What are the implications of my thinking?" For example, in a conversation about the salvific effect of the death of

Jesus, a participant might simply state that Jesus had to die for our sins. Through critical conversation—both the questions asked as well as the responses of other participants—a person might be encouraged to look more carefully at that statement and to ask where that concept came from and what it means in terms of how Jesus is seen as both fully divine and fully human.

Packed into a statement like "Jesus had to die for our sins" are all kinds of presumptions ("givens") about who Jesus is and who Jesus is for us. A conversation about this statement invites us to ask questions about Jesus' free will, about the role of his life and preaching, and about what we mean by salvation. Critical conversation can facilitate our looking and then looking again at these core underlying concepts and beliefs.

These three characteristics—sustained, engaged, and critical—mark the kind of conversations that nurture adult learning and enhance adult faith. But how do we nurture this kind of conversation? The answer is complex. On the one hand, developing the capacity for this kind of conversation among a group of adults takes time and patience. On the other hand, it can be facilitated with the use of trained facilitators and with the preparation of good questions.

Preparing Questions

Composing good questions that elicit the level of conversation that we seek is a skill that takes practice. The first step is to articulate what makes for a good question. Here are the descriptors that the World Café proposes as the basis for strong questions. "A powerful question is simple and clear, is thought provoking, generates energy, focuses inquiry, surfaces unconscious assumptions, and opens new possibilities."[10]

That is a tall order! It is important to begin by describing what the questions are designed to do—elicit a conversation about people's prior experience, prepare people for some common experience or ritual, project a different way of looking at the future. Where do you hope the emphasis of the conversation time is placed? Prepare your questions in light of that hope.

In any gathering, we can speak of questions falling into one of three categories:

OPENING INTRODUCTION: This is best done by going around the group, as it is important that each person have an opportunity to have their voice heard in the group. Saying "pass" is always an option. An "easy pitch" question can often set the foundation for the beginning of the conversation: "Introduce yourself and name an idea from the presentation that seemed new to you or that struck you in a new way." Or: "Name an experience during the past week (month, season) when you..." and select a common experience that connects with the theme of the conversation, such as "had a moment of silence" (beginning of a retreat), "felt like you were a good parent" (session for parents of children in first sacraments), or "heard a reading proclaimed really well at church" (beginning of a program for lectors).

MAKING LINKS: Here we want to begin the process of linking the content to people's experience, again always with an eye on the central, hoped-for focus of the conversation. "In the presentation (video/text) the point was made that....Has that been part of your experience or not? In what ways?"

TOWARD A FUTURE: The last set of questions points toward ways in which the topic being discussed can be brought to bear on the participants' lives. "How does the parish...? How might it improve?" or "How is this part of your family? What can you do this year to heighten your family's awareness of...?"

Once you have your questions prepared, review them with these questions in mind: [11]

- Is this question relevant to the lived experience of the people who will be exploring it?

- Is this a genuine question—a question to which I/we really don't know the answer?

- What assumptions or beliefs are embedded in the way this question is constructed?

- Is this question likely to generate hope, imagination, engagement, creative action, and new possibilities, or is it likely to increase a focus on past problems and obstacles?

- Does this question leave room for new and different questions to be raised as the initial question is explored?

As is clear from this discussion, creating good questions is hard work and is best done with a small team of people who can try out ideas together in the search for a question that will generate the kind of conversation that leads to living, explicit, and fruitful faith.

Questions for Reflection and Conversation

★ *Think about a time when you have been engaged in meaningful conversation with a small group of adults. What characterized that conversation? What contributed to its effectiveness? What works against that kind of conversation?*

★ *What do you find most challenging about planning and facilitating meaningful conversations among adults?*

Principles for Planning and Implementing Adult Programs

We have looked at the various characteristics that mark effective adult catechesis—rooting it in the experience of the adults, making connection between faith and life, creating a hospitable space, and working toward the potential of transformative learning. And we have seen that central to each of these is the call for sustained, engaged, critical conversation. It is in the context of conversation that we come to know our faith more clearly, learn to articulate it to others, and learn from the way in which others speak about their faith.

Bringing all of these variables together into a coherent and effective program for adults requires a good deal of work and the involvement of many. Here are some suggestions to get the process started.[12]

MAKE A COMMITMENT. If your parish believes that adult faith formation is important and says that lifelong learning is a priority, then the parish budget and resources need to reflect this. It is helpful to begin by naming what resources are presently being used to support your adult faith formation programs: financial resources, paid staff time, volunteer hours, etc. As you plan for a more vibrant program, make plans with the pastoral staff and pastoral council to begin to reallocate resources toward adult formation opportunities.

PICK A THEME: One model that has proved effective is for the pastoral team to decide on a theme for the year around which all adult formation experience will revolve. If a parish selects sacraments, for example, all aspects of parish programming would have that as a theme. A study group might read a book on the sacraments; the book club might use the lens of sacramentality of the world as the basis for choosing their books for the year. A retreat might be held for those caring for the elderly around the meaning of the sacrament of anointing. With a particular theme in mind, it is easier to create a sense of cohesion to the adult offerings, so that the whole parish is talking about and thinking about the same general topic.

INVOLVE AS MANY PEOPLE AS POSSIBLE. If you want to convey the importance of adult learning, then the entire pastoral team needs to be on deck—planning, evaluating, and leading. It is helpful to find ways for each member of the parish staff to contribute and participate in adult faith formation gatherings. If you don't have a large staff, find ways to involve members of the pastoral council or religious education committee.

PREPARE FACILITATORS. To create the opportunity for sustained, engaged, critical conversation, the role of trained facilitators is key. They often do more than simply lead the conversation; in their role of hosting a small group, they can be ambassadors for the pastoral staff. At the same time, most people working in religious education or faith formation are familiar with working with children and youth, so some instruction about how to respond to the needs of adults would be important. Having your facilitators preview the questions for conversation gives them a chance to reflect on them for themselves before they work with others.

PLAN YOUR TIME WELL. Well-planned sessions for adults include a rich interplay of prayer, presentation, conversation, and social time. As you think of the year's program, think of spending one-fourth of your time on each of these activities. That doesn't mean that the prayer for an hour session needs to be fifteen minutes; you can offer a retreat day that is almost all prayer and reflection and have shorter, though still well-planned, prayer experiences during other programs. One rule of thumb that is important to keep: the amount of time invested in conversation should be equal to or greater than the time allotted to presentation.

BE WELCOMING. Everything a parish does should be evangelizing, including the way in which we greet and welcome one another for an adult faith formation program. If the details of the event are done in advance, the pastoral staff is able to be present to the people who come. Keep in mind that this may be the first time a person has ventured into an adult faith formation program; making that a positive experience is important.

KEEP AN EYE ON THE LITURGICAL YEAR. When scheduling programs for adults, pay close attention to the liturgical seasons as an important dimension of parish life and a source of direction for planning. Integrating aspects of the liturgical symbols into the prayer for the adult formation program is helpful: using an Advent wreath during Advent, for example, or the color purple during Lent. When possible, it is effective to incorporate hymns, songs, and Scripture from a recent Sunday liturgy into the adult gathering. Look to Lent as an opportune time to offer a mini-series on a faith-related topic for adults or a special retreat.

DESSERT IS NOT OPTIONAL. Creating an atmosphere of welcome and hospitality almost always includes good food. If the program is in the morning, having coffee and tea available before and, if possible, during the program is very important. Having even the simplest dessert set out on trays adds to the feeling of hospitality. Be sure to have a selection of items for those with allergies or staying away from sweets.

To engage effectively in adult faith formation involves taking seriously the role of conversation. In so many ways, conversation is the linchpin to a process that contributes to transformative learning. Generating conversation can be challenging. Carefully preparing the questions and training facilitators to lead the conversation are important steps.

Keep in Mind

- Adults grow in their faith through a variety of experiences, both structured and intentional and informal and less intentional. Being aware of the diversity of these faith-fostering experiences is essential for effective adult faith formation.

- As we weave together intentional experiences of faith formation, four characteristics are present: that we begin with the experience of the adults, that we make the connection between faith and life, that we provide a hospitable space within which adults gather, and that all of these work together to form a context where transformative learning is possible.

- Conversation that is sustained, engaged, and critical is the most important component of effective adult faith formation. Through conversation we develop in our ability to articulate our own faith, which is enriched by hearing about the faith of others. This in turn leads to a living, explicit, and fruitful faith.

- Asking good questions, prepared in advance, is essential to effective conversation among adults.

Where we have looked at intentional programs for adults in this chapter, in chapter five we broaden our scope to look at the way in which the life of the faith community can itself be faith formative. What if we were to see each time adults gather—catechist meeting, choir practice, finance committee meeting—as an opportunity to enhance the faith life of the adults involved? That's what we examine in the next chapter.

CHAPTER FIVE

Community of Practice as Agent of Faith Formation

LOOK BACK AT THE STORIES THAT BEGAN CHAPTER three—Maryanne and the impact of the retreat and membership in the book club, Robert teaching fifth grade in the faith formation program, Bob and Margie and their work with a Katrina service trip. While each person's experience is different and the context that enhanced their faith is distinct, there is a common thread that runs through the stories: the formative impact of a small community of faith. In each account, the role of a small group within the parish was the context for strengthening the faith. For Maryanne, it was the retreat and belonging to the book club; for Robert, it was his engagement with a group of catechists that supported his faith; for Bob and Marge it was their working with a service project and ongoing membership in the social justice committee. That is the focus for this chapter—the way in which the various gathering of adults in our parishes can serve as an important context for fostering mature, adult faith.

Imagine for a moment a moderate-size parish with a moderate-size staff—a pastor, a catechetical leader, maybe a pastoral associate, and a part-time youth minister. If you were to look around this parish, you would note many different contexts in which adults gather; they might include the catechists, the RCIA team, the eucharistic ministers, the religious education committee, the social justice committee, the parish council, and the Tuesday AM Bible study. I am proposing here that we look more carefully at these various groups and at the multiple contexts in which adults gather within the parish as opportunities to foster the faith of the members. We can refer to these groups as "communities of practice"[1]: they are gatherings of people engaged in various practices that contribute to the group's goals and that shape the identity and faith of the members.

When we speak of a community of practice, how is the term "practice" understood? Practice here refers not so much to the individual activities or practices of a given group but to the broader endeavor in which they are involved. We often speak of a law practice or a medical practice, by which we refer to the gathering of people who engage in the endeavors of law or medicine. They are practitioners of law or medicine. In a similar way when we speak of communities of practice we are referring to a gathering of practitioners. The catechists form a community around being practitioners of catechesis. The RCIA team forms a community of practitioners around the work of initiation. Practice here refers to the broad endeavor within which our activities and experiences are meaningful.

What I am proposing here is that each of these communities

of practice—through the activities or practices in which they engage and the way they engage these practices—can serve as an essential component of adult faith formation.

Communities of Practice

Our parishes are made up of groups of people gathered around areas of interest and responsibility that shape the life of the parish. Thinking of them as communities of practice allows us to see them in a somewhat different light. In addition to accomplishing tasks, these small communities can serve as important vehicles for shaping the life and vision of the parish and contributing to the faith formation of adults. To look at this more closely, I begin with a series of propositions about the nature and dynamics of these parish groups and committees when seen through the lens of communities of practice. Then, after looking at one group as it functions as a community of practice, I outline ways in which we can heighten the faith formative nature of these communities.

THE ENTERPRISE OF EACH COMMUNITY IS BROADER THAN ITS SEPARATE TASKS. [2] Each time one of these groups meets, it has a particular task to accomplish: the catechists might meet for training or to plan the next set of sessions for their grade level or to discuss a multigenerational gathering planned for Advent; the parish council meets to discuss how to welcome and integrate into parish life the rising number of Spanish-speaking immigrants; the finance committee meets to discuss the parish budget. And the list goes on.

At the same time that each group has a particular task to accomplish at a specific meeting, there is also an overarching "charge" or responsibility to the wider parish that each group is to address. For example, as a group, the catechists are responsible for the formal catechesis of the adults, children, and youth of the parish. While it might be easy at times to lose track of that larger responsibility in the details of class lists, adult session themes, and grade level liturgies, nonetheless, to be a catechist is to be a participant in this larger responsibility. Members of the parish council are charged with the task on helping the pastor prioritize the pastoral needs of the parish. That is the overarching responsibility of the group that takes the form of smaller tasks and activities that serve the needs of the parish. So each group within the parish has a particular role to play in the life of the community, which it accomplishes with greater or lesser success.

And I would go one step further and propose that each of these groups participates in the larger mission of the parish, which is to be and become an ever more effective agent of evangelization.

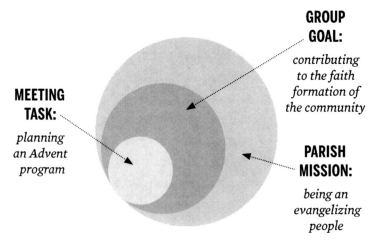

GROUP GOAL:
contributing to the faith formation of the community

MEETING TASK:
planning an Advent program

PARISH MISSION:
being an evangelizing people

So a parish is made up of a number of smaller groups through which the work of the parish is accomplished. The groups meet with some regularity to address specific tasks that are part of their general charge or responsibility, which is itself part of the larger mission of an evangelizing parish.

THE COMMUNITY'S ENTERPRISE SHAPES THE GROUP AND THE GROUP SHAPES THE EXPRESSION OF THE ENTERPRISE. Communities do not develop in theory; they evolve in response to a particular focus of interest or a specific goal. The members of the RCIA team gather to enhance their ability to share faith with potential new members and to help form the candidates and catechumens in the Catholic faith. Several youth ministers from neighboring parishes gather regularly because of their dedication to their work with youth and to their own faith lives. A group of parents of young children gathers monthly for conversation and support with a particular interest in strengthening the faith life of their children and families. Each of these groups—or communities—is rooted in a shared enterprise, a corporate endeavor to which the members are committed.

The shared enterprise defines the scope and focus on the work of the members of the community; it delineates the group's range of responsibility. The community of practice develops as a function of the participation of the members in this shared enterprise. At the same time that the community develops in light of the shared enterprise, the shape of that enterprise is defined by the members of the community. The nature and direction of the enterprise only becomes clear in the doing. Consider an RCIA team, for example. At some level, the task to which they are committed is one that is shared by most RCIA teams: invite those who are interested in joining the Catholic Church to an extended conversation where questions are addressed, faith is shared, and the core teachings of the church are made accessible. But the way that the group's work is given expression is determined by the actual involvement of this particular team in the common task. The understanding of the goal of each session, the integration of prayer and reflection on Scripture, the particular resources that are used, the approach to leadership, and the connection with the wider parish—all of these elements take shape in actually doing the shared enterprise. So while the enterprise may be defined at some level from outside the community of practice itself and may be understood only in light of the parish of which it is a part, its shape and expression are the results of the participation of the members. The scope and limits of the shared enterprise of a particular community of practice is a dynamic reality formed and reformed in the doing of the work.

PARTICIPATION IN A COMMUNITY OF PRACTICE SHAPES THE IDENTITY AND WORLDVIEW OF THE MEMBERS. Robert teaches fifth-grade faith formation; he will be the first to admit that he has learned as much as his students about the church and the sacraments. Beyond learning facts about church teaching, he has also gained new perspective on his role in the church and his place in the parish. Participating with other catechists in monthly meetings where they gather for prayer, reflection, and conversation about the themes of the upcoming sessions has renewed Robert's faith. Even when Robert is not serving as a catechist, his belonging to the community of catechists[3] is part of his identity; it shapes how he makes meaning of the world around him. He consciously and unconsciously hears the homily on Sunday and the evening news during the week through the perspective gained as a participant in the catechists' community of practice.

Our identity is shaped in part by who we are as participants in the various communities of practice. It is the intertwining of our multiple-memberships in the communities of practice that shape our lives. We identify *with* and *as* members of particular communities of practice. Who we are and who we become are influenced by the communities of practice of which we are members. The practices within a particular community get incorporated in how we engage with the world around us. Participating in the enterprise that is at the heart of the community of practice among the catechists has given Robert new knowledge, skills, and tools for understanding perspectives and ideas that are different from his own. The opportunity for prayer, reflection, and conversation that he has experienced within this community has influence beyond his job as a catechist. It has an impact on the way he raises his children, goes about his business life, and thinks and acts as a citizen.

THE PARISH IS MADE UP OF A NUMBER OF COMMUNITIES OF PRACTICE THROUGH WHICH THE WORK OF THE PARISH IS DONE; WE CAN THINK OF THE PARISH AS A CONSTELLATION OF COMMUNITIES OF PRACTICE. Just as a constellation is constituted by the stars that make it up, so the parish is shaped by the communities of practice within it. The stars get their definition and sense of place from their setting within the constellation; similarly, the communities of practice within a parish gain their meaning and mission from their role within the faith community.

While each community of practice within the constellation of the parish—the RCIA team, the youth ministry advisory board, the liturgy committee—has its own task or enterprise, it also participates in the work of the parish: being and becoming an ever more effective agent of evangelization and shaping its members for that task. So the "success" of a community of practice rests not only in its effectiveness in engaging in its shared enterprise; it is also about addressing the enterprise embodied in the constellation. In the case of a community that is part of a parish as constellation, this means that it is responsible for its own enterprise and for enhancing the faith life of its members so that they can more effectively proclaim the gospel in action and word.

Thinking of the parish as a constellation of communities of practice can contribute to a context that works against the "silo thinking" that shapes many parishes. It can be frustrating working in a parish when groups—youth ministers, catechists, school leadership, choir, RCIA team—are each functioning without reference to the other groups. This silo thinking contributes to a lack of a shared vision and takes away from the parish's ability to really be a clear agent of evangelization. If we pay more attention to the groups that gather in our parishes and recognize them as communities of practice that participate in the constellation of communities of practice that make up the parish, there is the potential for overcoming the separatist view. Many people are in multiple communities of practice; as they claim their membership in their various communities of practice, they can come to see their role as mediators between the communities. Perhaps someone is a member of the RCIA team and also in the choir. She or he serves as an intermediary between the two communities, making their working relationship more effective. Bringing to the choir a deeper understanding of the various rites of the RCIA can heighten the choir's participation and engagement with these parts of the liturgy.

By Way of Example

Here is an example of a community of practice and how it has unfolded over time. A group of six women form the community of practice responsible for the weekly Liturgy of the Word for Children (LWC) at the 9:30 Sunday liturgy.

It is important to note that it would be possible, though I think less effective, to facilitate these LWCs without being a community of practice: a group of six people could meet every few months to divvy up the weeks, take care of logistics, and receive the published material that would be the basis of each person running their own LWC on their assigned week. While we might be able to say that this group had a shared endeavor, it is not being shaped and reshaped by the participation of the members. But in the case described here, they do form a community of practice that functions effectively.

Those responsible for the LWC meet every two weeks. They hold in common a sense of a shared enterprise, which has developed some over the past few years. Where, in the beginning, it was exclusively focused on what they needed to do for the children, over time it has evolved to include attention to their own engagement with the Sunday readings and thus to their own faith development. This shift began as a suggestion from the parish catechetical leader when she met with the group to discuss some new resources that had been published. However, the way that shift evolved was shaped by the group members.

The members take the biweekly meetings as a serious commitment and are present for most meetings, and in most cases they have reviewed in advance the Sunday readings for the next two weeks. Over the time of working together they have come to respect one another's gifts and appreciate the diversity with which they approach their tasks. In recent months, they have had a new member join the group. A mother of two young children, she had recently moved into the parish and had heard about the LWC through the parish's monthly Welcome Night that she had attended with her husband. Her involvement with this group is one of the primary ways she has come to experience the parish as home.

While by no means rigid in structure, there is a basic rhythm to their meetings. They spend some time catching up on one another's lives and then proceed to do a reflection on the gospel readings for the next two Sundays, talking about the implications that these readings have for their own lives. Only when that is completed do they begin discussing the children's program: reviewing what happened well and not so well over the prior couple of weeks, discussing themes that they might want to highlight for the upcoming Sundays, deciding on the process they will use, and dividing up the tasks. Over the past few months they have gotten in the habit of using the last few minutes of the meeting to talk about concerns they might have in their family or work life and asking one another for prayers. This is a new activity being added to their usual meeting routine.

As an intentional community of practice, the group that meets to plan the Liturgy of the Word for Children accomplishes several things. In addition to planning the sessions for children they also enhance the faith life of those in the planning group itself. In many ways, this group participates in the larger mission of the parish to be an evangelizing agent in the church and in the world.

Groups of adults already gather in our parish communities for a variety of reasons and to accomplish a diversity of tasks. Seeing them as potential communities of practice invites parish leaders to recognize the role they can play in fostering the goals and vision of the parish and enhancing the faith life of the members.

For Reflection and Conversation

★ *Think about a community of practice of which you are a participant–both within and outside the parish. Reflect on what you see to be the goal or core endeavor of this group. In what ways has that changed or been reinterpreted over time? How has your membership in the group shaped your own identity or sense of yourself?*

★ *Think about a group in your pastoral setting that functions well. In what ways does thinking of it as a community of practice help you to understand its effectiveness and the influence it has within the parish? How about for those communities of practice that are less effective?*

Being Intentional About Communities of Practice
Looking at the groups and committees that make up the life of the parish through the lens of communities of practice provides us with some practical insights into how groups function and what makes groups effective.

But the potential for these communities of practice to contribute to the maturing faith of the whole parish rests in the intentionality with which the communities are engaged and sustained. I believe we need to be intentional about articulating and embracing the faith dimension of each of the parish's communities of practice, recognizing the communities of practice as the essential resource in welcoming new members and renewing established members, incorporating a process of discernment in order to engage people's gifts most effectively, and seeing the communities of practice as the context for introducing parish-wide initiatives that support the faith formation of the whole parish, particularly the adults. Let's examine each of these.

THE FAITH DIMENSION

Some of the most task-oriented groups in a parish are the most efficient, attending to their responsibilities with alacrity and competence. But are those necessarily the most effective at integrating the faith dimension into their endeavors and fostering the faith life of their members? Whether we are talking about the youth ministry advisory board or the finance committee, the RCIA team or the ushers, each group in a parish is called to integrate into their work the overall mission of the church—to be and become an ever more effective agent of evangelization. To do that, it is the responsibility of each group, within their area of expertise, to bring into focus the three-fold dimension of our faith: relationship with Jesus, affiliation with the Christian community, and participation in the church's mission.[4] While the social justice committee might be emphasizing the church's mission to the world, and the ushers might be focusing on affiliation with the Christian community, in the final analysis, each time a group of adults of the parish gather, there is a call to attend to the growth in faith of the whole parish. One of the primary ways for communities of practice to foster the faith of the whole parish is to attend to the faith life of its members.

The shared enterprise of each effective community of practice involves three levels. The first is the fundamental role or responsibility that they have in the parish—the faith formation of adults, children, or youth; the planning, implementing, and evaluating of the parish's liturgical life; or the welcoming and formation of new members. At a second level, each community has responsibility to the overall mission of the parish—to further the work of evangelization. And to do that successfully, each community of practice also has the responsibility of taking seriously the task of fostering the faith life of its members.

What would it look like if each community of practice in a parish understood the shared enterprise of the group to include the faith development of its members? Including meaningful prayer, time for reflection and conversation about the Sunday's readings, or retreat evenings are all ways to attend to the faith of a community's members. It is important to see these as integral to the task of the group, rather than as an "extra"; time for prayer and reflection doesn't get set aside or greatly reduced when the community of practice is faced with a particularly heavy agenda. A rule of thumb: over the course of a year, twenty or twenty-five percent of the committee's meeting time might be given over to this crucial dimension of its work.

RESOURCE IN WELCOMING

While we often use the term "parish community," most of our parishes are simply too large to be communities in any meaningful way. Their size makes mutual engagement across the whole parish impossible; their complexity precludes the possibilities of members being able to grasp, much less participate in, a single, shared enterprise. In reality, those who truly "belong" to the parish—those for whom the parish has some element of influence on their faith and on how they see the world—belong to some smaller part of the parish, some community of practice. In most parishes, repeated in many different versions, this would be the story: we went to Mass on Sunday, but didn't really feel a part of the parish until my children were school-age and I got involved in religious education; or until I became a member of the social justice committee because of its work with the homeless; or until I joined the choir; or until a friend invited me to join the parish book club, and I got really involved in that.

Recognizing the importance of connecting with communities of practice for the sense of affiliation with the parish, it would be helpful to see these communities as resources for connecting new or renewing members with the life of the parish. There is often one of two responses to new "recruits" by a group or committee in a parish: either they are brought in and quickly put to work—say, teaching third-grade faith formation—with only the briefest explanation of the practical side of things, or the welcome is less than generous, and no one seems to pay them much attention as they struggle to find a place in the group. In neither case is there a real sense of welcome and hospitality. Establishing a process by which new members are brought into the community of practice, integrated into the ways of the group, and given appropriate tasks and responsibilities is essential to effective and vital communities.

A genuine community of practice is most effective when there is a continuous flow of some people coming into a community, while others are moving from peripheral roles to leadership positions, and others are moving out of that particular ministry in an expansion of their expressions of discipleship. This type of movement makes for healthy, vital communities of practice and works against any tendency toward them becoming cliques or one person's fiefdom.

PROCESS OF DISCERNMENT

Not everyone can successfully facilitate conversation with adults; for some, the idea of working with youth is really uninviting; visiting the sick takes a special kind of person. It is the responsibility of each of us and of the parish as a whole to draw on the God-given strengths and gifts of each person so as most effectively to respond to God's invitation to partnership in the ongoing work of furthering the reign of God. Ideally, within a community of practice, the gifts of each member are recognized, appreciated, and supported, because in an effective community of practice (again, ideally), each person's gifts contribute to the mutual engagement around the shared enterprise.

Establishing a process by which people's gifts can be named is an important part of effective leadership of a parish and a central element of establishing dynamic communities of practice. This can be as simple as having the opportunity to sit down with someone to talk about what you're good at or what you enjoy doing. Having someone in the parish serve as a "broker" for people who wish to engage more fully in the life of the parish would be a good starting point. Perhaps the welcoming process for new members of the parish could include some time to discern where their gifts might best be used in the parish and beyond.

ADULT FAITH FORMATION INITIATIVES

Many models of adult faith formation emphasize the importance of having core experiences that members of the parish can hold in common. Whether these are large multigenerational gatherings around a liturgical season or something as simple as printing in the bulletin each week a common question to guide reflection on the Sunday's gospel, these opportunities to share in a common experience are valued in many approaches to lifelong faith formation. The communities of practice within a parish provide an already existing forum through which these types of experience can be organized.

Perhaps there is an agreement that all groups and committees will begin each meeting with some sharing on the Sunday's gospel. Or maybe each week a different community takes responsibility for hosting a simple Lenten dinner as part of an adult program. In whatever ways, complex or simple, the communities of practice within a parish can serve as a helpful context for initiating some opportunities.

In each of these four intentional focuses, what is being called for is a shifting of the shared enterprise of each of the communities of practice from an exclusively pragmatic emphasis, such as planning the next youth retreat, or practicing new songs to sing for Sunday's liturgy. The shift is toward a broader understanding of the shared enterprise to include explicit attention to the faith dimension and to the faith life of the communities' members.

Questions for Reflection and Conversation

★ *What would it look like if each community of practice in a parish understood the shared enterprise of the group to include the faith development of its members? What would be some basic practices one might introduce to address this?*

★   *Imagine that the various communities of practice in a parish are the first line of welcome for new or renewing members. What are some ways to make that happen in your own pastoral setting?*

★   *In what ways are people in your parish given the opportunity to examine and name their gifts and how they might be used within the parish? How might this be enhanced?*

★   *How might the various groups and communities within the parish serve as a context or forum within which to introduce common faith formation experiences shared by the whole parish?*

Keep in Mind

Adults regularly gather in the parish for a variety of reasons; each of these gatherings can be an opportunity to foster the faith life of the adults and enhance their ability to be and become ever more effective evangelizers.

*   Establishing the various gathering of adults within our parish as "communities of practice" involves attending to the three elements of the group's work: the specific task of the meeting, the wider responsibility of the group, and the group's connection to the mission of the parish to be an evangelizing agent.

*   Communities of practice serve as important contexts for welcoming new or renewing members into the life of the parish.

*   Most parishes are too large to be considered a community of practice; we can think of them as constellations of com-

munities of practice. It is through the mission and vision of the parish that the communities within the parish gain their identity and direction.

- Membership in communities of practice forms our identity; our experience within the community has the potential of shaping our view of the world.

Final thought

To understand our parishes through the lens of communities of practice is to invite the adults and leaders of the parish to rethink the way we gather and the work we do. That can seem like a daunting task. Let me share with you a piece of advice I received when I first started doing parish work. Convinced of the need to change the focus of faith formation from children to adults, I was overwhelmed by the challenges of bringing such a vision into reality. My pastor, encouraging of my work and supportive of its direction, heard my frustration and gave me great guidance. "Remember, if you can't move in the right direction, at least lean that way!" Let's together all lean into the reality of an adult church eagerly engaged in the mission of evangelization.

CHAPTER 1

1 All Scripture quotes are from *New American Bible*, Revised Edition (NABRE). Available at http://www.usccb.org/bible/

2 See Luke 14:15–24; Mark 4:1–20; Luke 15:8–10

3 See Luke 15:11–32; Luke 15:4–7; Luke 10:25–37

4 See Mark 6:7–13

5 Further discussion on these characteristics can be found in Jane Regan, *Toward an Evangelizing Church* (Washington, DC: NCEA, 2003). See also Harold Horell, "Cultural Postmodernity and Christian Faith Formation." In Thomas Groome and Harold Horell (eds.) *Horizons and Hopes: The Future of Religious Education* (Mahwah, NJ: Paulist Press, 2003) 83-89.

6 *General Catechetical Directory* (GCD – 1971). Washington, DC: USCC, 1971. Available at http://www.vatican.va/roman_curia/congregations/cclergy/documents/rc_con_cclergy_doc_11041971_gcat_en.html

7 Pope Paul VI, *Evangelii Nuntiandi* (EN), "Apostolic Exhortation on Evangelization" (1975). Available at http://www.vatican.va/holy_father/paul_vi/apost_exhortations/documents/hf_p-vi_exh_19751208_evangelii-nuntiandi_en.html

---

CHAPTER 2

1 Pope Paul VI, *Evangelii Nuntiandi* (EN), "Apostolic Exhortation on Evangelization" (1975). Accessed at http://www.vatican.va/holy_father/paul_vi/apost_exhortations/documents/hf_p-vi_exh_19751208_evangelii-nuntiandi_en.html

2 Pray-As-You-Go is a Jesuit initiative to provide Scripture reflection for people to download and use when travelling to work. It can be accessed at http://www.jesuit.org.uk/jmi/pray-as-you-go.htm

3   *Ad Gentes* (AG), "On the Missionary Activity of the Church" (1965). Accessed at http://www.vatican.va/archive/hist_councils/ii_vatican_council/documents/vat-ii_decree_19651207_ad-gentes_en.html

4   Pope John Paul II, *Catechesi Tradendae* (CT), "Apostolic Exhortation on Catechesis" (1979). Accessed at http://www.vatican.va/holy_father/john_paul_ii/apost_exhortations/documents/hf_jp-ii_exh_16101979_catechesi-tradendae_en.html

5   Pope John Paul II, *Christifideles Laici* (CL), "Apostolic Exhortation on the Laity" (1988). Accessed at http://www.vatican.va/holy_father/john_paul_ii/apost_exhortations/documents/hf_jp-ii_exh_30121988_christifideles-laici_en.html

6   Pope John Paul II, *Redemptoris Missio* (RM), "On the Church's Mission Activity" (1990). Accessed at http://www.vatican.va/holy_father/john_paul_ii/encyclicals/documents/hf_jp-ii_enc_07121990_redemptoris-missio_en.html

7   Congregation for the Clergy, General Directory for Catechesis (1998). Accessed at http://www.vatican.va/roman_curia/congregations/cclergy/documents/rc_con_ccatheduc_doc_17041998_directory-for-catechesis_en.html

8   For background on the genre of directory and an analysis of this document, see Jane E Regan and Michael P. Horan, *Good News in New Forms*. (Washington, DC: National Conference of Catechetical Leaders, 2000).

9   "Message to the People of God," 2012. Accessed at http://www.vatican.va/roman_curia/synod/documents/rc_synod_doc_20121026_message-synod_en.html

10   Pope Francis, *Evangelii Gaudium* (EG) "The Joy of the Gospel" (2013). Accessed at http://www.vatican.va/holy_father/francesco/apost_exhortations/documents/papa-francesco_esortazione-ap_20131124_evangelii-gaudium_en.html

11   Congregation for the Clergy, *General Catechetical Directory* (1971). Accessed at http://www.vatican.va/roman_curia/congregations/cclergy/documents/rc_con_cclergy_doc_11041971_gcat_en.html

12 The International Council on Catechesis, a committee within the Congregation for the Clergy, met in 1988 to discuss adult catechesis. This document, "Adult Catechesis in the Christian Community," (1990) was a summary of the results of that meeting. Available at http://www.vatican. va/roman_curia/congregations/cclergy/documents/rc_con_cclergy_ doc_14041990_acat_en.html

---

CHAPTER 3

1 See *Evangelii Nuntiandi*, 14.

2 In her book *Fashion Me a People: Curriculum in the Church* (Louisville, KY: Westminster, 1989), Maria Harris proposes that the forms through which the church is constituted—preaching, teaching, service, liturgy, and community—serve as the content and context of catechesis. As she writes, "Education in the church means taking those forms which ecclesial life presents to us, places in our hands, as clay to be molded. Education is the work of lifting out those forms through which we might refashion ourselves into a pastoral people" (41). This is discussed in detail in chapter five.

3 USCCB, *Our Hearts Were Burning Within Us: A Pastoral Plan for Adult Faith Formation in the United States* (Washington, DC: USCC, 1999). Available at http://old.usccb.org/education/ourhearts.htm#part2a

4 This description of faith is taken from the *GDC*, which states: "Catechesis is that particular form of the ministry of the word which matures initial conversion to make it into a living, explicit and fruitful confession of faith" (GDC 82).

5 This theme is echoed across most of the documents on catechesis that we have been discussing. See, for example, the *Catechism of the Catholic Church* (CCC), 426; GDC, 36-43; and OHWB, 68.

6 There is a plethora of good resources for group Bible studies available from various publishers. Here, just to name a few: from Twenty-Third Publications is the *Threshold Bible Study* series, which is a thematic Scripture study program, designed for both personal study and group discussion. For information: http://store.pastoralplanning.com/thbist1. html; from Loyola Press comes *Six Week with the Bible*, a series of Scripture studies that are both thematic and based on various books of the Bible. These are specifically designed for Catholics and can be used as either individual study or small group Bible study. For information: http://www.loyolapress.com/six-weeks-with-the-bible-series.htm. Published by Liturgical Press, the **Little Rock Bible Study** provides a range of Bible studies for beginners through advanced. Each Bible study includes a text and a study guide. For information: http://www.littlerockscripture.org/en/programs.html

7   Online courses and workshops focusing on the gospels are available through C21 Online from the School of Theology and Ministry at Boston College. For information: http://www.bc.edu/c21online/

8   The series from Twenty-Third Publications as well as from Loyola Press are appropriate for personal Bible study. For daily reflections on the Scriptures of the day, I propose two options: **Pray-as-you-Go**, audio reflections you can download to your MP3 player or your iPad; they run about 10 minutes and include music, Scripture, reflection, and silence. Information at: http://www.pray-as-you-go.org/. Also, Loyola Press publishes an annual reflection on the daily readings, **A Book of Grace-Filled Days**.

9   The approach to lectio divina is taken from a presentation given by Thomas Groome and Colleen Griffith on October 16, 2012. Available at http://www.bc.edu/content/bc/church21/webcast.html. See also Schneiders, Sandra, "Lectio Divina: Transformative Engagement with Scripture" in Thomas Groome and Colleen Griffith (eds), **Catholic Spiritual Practices: A Treasury of Old and New**, 117-119. (Brewster, MA: Paraclete Press, 2012).

10   Pew Research Center reports 41% of Americans say they attend church regularly; studies that are based on head count and other forms of data collection put the number closer to 30%.

11   Participation in planning, implementing, and evaluating liturgy is itself a helpful form of adult faith formation.

12   These might also be good opportunities to ask people why they don't attend. Couched in terms of missing seeing them at Mass, people may well welcome an opportunity to talk about why they stopped attending.

13   This concept of balancing memory and openness is further developed in Jane Regan and Mimi Bitzan, **What Does It Mean to Be Catholic?** (Chicago: Loyola Press, 2005), 89-96

14 This idea of the fundamental relationship between memory and openness is articulated well by Lawrence Cunningham in *The Catholic Experience* (New York: Crossroads, 1985). See particularly the chapter "Catholicity."

15 Hebrews 4:14-16

16 Here I am drawing on Harris, *Fashion Me a People*, where she uses this term to refer to the kingly role of the Christian. Care needs to be taken, however, that we not mistakenly equate the term political with partisanship or political parties. Here it simply refers to the way in which the particular gathering of people is organized and led.

17 "Sharing Catholic Social Teaching: Challenges and Directions" accessible at http://www.usccb.org/beliefs-and-teachings/what-we-believe/catholic-social-teaching/sharing-catholic-social-teaching-challenges-and-directions.cfm

18 NCCB, *Economic Justice for All* (Washington, DC: USCC, 1986). Available at: http://www.usccb.org/upload/economic_justice_for_all.pdf

---

CHAPTER 4

1 I use intergenerational to refer to programs offered with children and adults together: for example, a retreat for children preparing for first sacraments and their parents. When referring to a parish's programs that include intergenerational as well as peer gatherings, I prefer "multi-generational" as a broader and more inclusive term.

2 By peer-group gatherings I mean those programs offered for a particular group. Among the adult community this could include the gatherings of young adults or of parents of children receiving first sacraments. It could also include programs for those providing care for elderly parents or for women alone or men alone.

3 In *Blessed Rage for Order* (New York: Seabury Press, 1975), David Tracy points to the "limit experiences" in our lives as the indicators of the religious or transcendent in human experience. He writes: "Such features can be analyzed as both expressive of certain 'limits-to' our ordinary experience (e.g., finitude, contingency, or radical transience) and disclosive of certain fundamental structures of our existence beyond (or, alternatively, grounding to) that ordinary experience (e.g., our fundamental trust in the worthwhileness of existence, our basic belief in order and value)."

4   These themes were originally developed as part of *We Celebrate the Eucharist* program designed by Christiane Brusselmans and published by Silver Burdett beginning in the mid-1970s. In many ways, with its emphasis on the interplay of catechesis and liturgy, on the importance of adult catechesis, and on experiential learning, it anticipated and contributed to later developments in intergenerational catechesis.

5   This is the basic thesis behind the book by Groome, *Will There Be Faith? A New Vision for Educating and Growing Disciples* (San Francisco: Harper One, 2011).

6   Parker J. Palmer, *To Know as We Are Known: A Spirituality of Education* (San Francisco: Harper and Row, 1983), 74.

7   Jane E. Regan, *Toward an Adult Church: A Vision of Faith Formation* (Chicago: Loyola Press, 2002), 89-92.

8   Hans-Georg Gadamer, *Truth and Method*, second edition (New York: Continuum, 1989), 385.

9   David Tracy, *The Analogical Imagination: Christian Theology and the Culture of Pluralism* (New York: Crossroads, 1981), 101.

10   The World Café describes itself as "a powerful social technology for engaging people in conversations that matter, offering an effective antidote to the fast-paced fragmentation and lack of connection in today's world." (http://www.theworldcafe.com/about.html) Providing the framework for conversation in various settings around the world, the World Café is a helpful resource in encouraging conversation and good questions. This description of powerful questions appears in Juanita Brown, David Isaacs, Eric Vogt, and Nancy Margulies, "Strategic Questioning: Engaging People's Best Thinking" Systems Thinker 13 (9) 2002: 2-6. Accessed at: http://www. theworldcafe.com/articles/strategicquestion.pdf

11   These questions are adapted from Sally Roth, *Public Conversations Project*, 1998, in Juanita Brown, David Isaacs, Eric Vogt, and Nancy Margulies, "Strategic Questioning: Engaging People's Best Thinking."

12 This is adapted from Jane Regan and Mimi Bitzan, *What Does It Mean to Be Catholic?* (Chicago: Loyola Press, 2005), 21-28.

CHAPTER 5

1 Here I am drawing on the work of Etienne Wenger and particularly his book *Communities of Practice: Learning, Meaning, and Identity* (Cambridge University Press, 2000). In this book Wenger examines the place of communities of practice in the context of business. At the heart of his argument is that it is through communities of practice that knowledge is shared, identities are formed, and the work of the organization gets most effectively completed.

2 According to Wenger, one of the three key characteristics that mark communities of practice is the shared enterprise. It is in participating in this shared enterprise that the community is formed and membership defined. The other two key characteristics are mutual engagement and common repertoire.

3 It is important to note that simply being catechists in the same parish does not constitute a community of practice. In many parishes, the catechists have little engagement with one another; they come in for the assigned classes and may have little or no contact with other catechists. The group that Robert meets with monthly is a community of practice that furthers the group's work and shapes the identity of its members.

4 These three dimensions of the Christian life are discussed in chapter 1 and again in chapter 3 when they are considered as the fundamental goals of adult faith formation.

Disciples of All Nations
*Your Guide to Living and Understanding
the New Evangelization*
DR. JOSEPHINE LOMBARDI

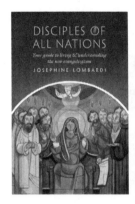

Scholar, author, and popular workshop leader Dr. Josephine Lombardi examines Catholic teaching on evangelization; its history, and theology; and how the New Evangelization influences everything from politics, culture, and social media to personal relationships and our own self-perception. With reflection/discussion questions and a detailed study guide. **176 PAGES | $16.95 | 9781627850223**

An Invitation to Catholic Faith
Exploring the Basics
JOSEPH STOUTZENBERGER

In clear and concise language, the author explains Catholic approaches to Scripture, Tradition, the sacraments, spiritual practices, and more. Wise and lively commentary plus discussion questions make this book perfect for individual or group study; for RCIA inquirers, catechumens, candidates, and for returning or practicing Catholics.
176 PP | $16.95 | 9781585959167

Dreams and Visions
Pastoral Planning for Lifelong Faith Formation
BILL HUEBSCH

Here Bill urges parish leaders and ministers to move in the direction of lifelong faith formation by offering parishioners powerful conversion experiences. He also offers a clear and consistent plan for step-by-step growth, with special emphasis on excellent liturgies, strong and effective catechist and teacher formation, and developing households of faith. **160 PAGES | $14.95 | 9781585956388**

1-800-321-0411
WWW.23RDPUBLICATIONS.COM

TWENTY
THIRD
PUBLICATIONS